Beyond Death & Taxes

A Guide to Total Wealth Control

GREGORY J. ENGLUND
ATTORNEY AT LAW

Estate planning is an individual and personal matter for each person and his or her family. Current fmancial circumstances and long-term financial goals differ, as do relationships among family members. Tax laws are subject to interpretation and frequent revision. For all these reasons, this book is not intended to be a substitute for personal tax and legal advice. No reader should undertake any of the suggestions described in this book without first consulting competent professional advisors.

Nineteenth Printing

Printed in the United States of America

Library of Congress Catalog Card Number: 93-94045

ISBN 0-9636401-0-0

Gregory J. Englund, Esq.
101 Federal Street, Suite 650
Boston, MA 02110
(617) 439-6796

Email: GJEnglund@EnglundLawFirm.com

Special bulk rates for the purchase of Beyond Death & Taxes are available. Please contact Mr. Englund for details.

TABLE OF CONTENTS

INTRODUCTION

For many people the somewhat nebulous subject of estate planning can be compressed to that familiar, fatalistic phrase: death and taxes. Nothing in life is certain but Death and Taxes.

During my more than thirty years in the law I have worked closely with clients to ease the burden of these twin fates. I have drafted Wills and Trusts. I have helped clients select guardians, executors and trustees. I have worked as part of a team with other attorneys, accountants, insurance agents, financial advisors, trust officers and charitable organizations, to build and preserve investments, to provide for the continuity of family businesses, to save family lands from the bulldozer, to support worthy causes. The results have been very positive.

Still, after all is said and done, there is a philosophical shrug of the shoulders. We have done all that can be done for the clients' estate plans. Now the clients are ready... for Death and Taxes.

That was then.

In recent years I have come to agree with Mark Twain, an early estate planner: the inevitability of estate taxes and other taxes triggered by death has been greatly exaggerated.

Using familiar planning techniques in new ways, and working with colleagues in many professional disciplines, we have been building an approach to planning that I call **Total Wealth Control.** One variation of this approach, known as the **Zero Estate Tax Plan**, allows clients to eliminate all federal estate tax. *The process* is referred to as the **New Estate Planning.**

What about the other eternal fate, death? The medical profession has made great advances on the frontiers of mortality. Today's newspaper supplies the latest evidence for the increasing length of life. Still, you remain resigned to the reality that your life will one day come to rest. Or will it? What if there were a way to let the ideals of your life live on, to create new opportunity for the qualities that make life worth living? To educate the next generation of children? To fund medical research? To support the arts? To provide decent housing? To train workers for satisfying jobs? To protect our environment? To sustain our religious organizations?

"Yes, of course," you are thinking. "You are talking about philanthropy, about creating a vehicle that can carry on the charitable values of individuals and their families."

That would be a kind of immortality: to transform your highest values and your worldly goods into a program of good works that continue long after you pass from this earth.

"Fine and noble," you agree, "but I am not a philanthropist."

That may be wistful realism. For many clients, that was the old answer to the eternal question of mortality.

Now let's consider a new answer — starting with your own situation.

When you or your spouse die, will there be an estate tax due? For tens of thousands of Americans, the answer is Yes. You may very well be among these Americans, even if you have done "state of the art" estate planning. A heavy tax bill hangs over you and your family: $500,000 or more.

These Americans are the **involuntary philanthropists**. When they die, their families will send enormous sums to the tax collectors.

Although estate taxes can easily crush a specific family, such taxes are but a drop in the ocean of the federal and state budgets, quickly spent and forgotten. What if those same dollars could be held in a fund, to be preserved, and applied by you and your family to specific charitable programs of your choosing? This is **voluntary philanthropy.** *You and your family control all of your wealth.*

Imagine the possibilities. Please, close your eyes for a moment or two and deliver your tax dollars to another fate... What programs have you always wished you could create or support, to benefit the people in your Community? What would you like to return to your Community? How would you like to be remembered in your Community?

Thank you. That effort was very important, because you now have at least one **VISION** of what your choices might mean, what difference you might make if only you could find the resources.

With the expert assistance of your planning advisors, perhaps you have determined that if you and your spouse were both to die today, your combined estate taxes would be less than $500,000 (or whatever other amount you may consider to be "significant"). If that is so, why should you be interested in the New Estate Planning? Please remember that planning is a dynamic process; actually, it may be more accurate to say that planning forces are always at work, like the wind and the waves.

To illustrate the power of just one of these forces, you may use a handy device known as the **Rule of 72**. Example: You and your spouse are age 40. Your combined estates, including life insurance proceeds and retirement plan benefits, have a value of $3,000,000. Realizing that your estates may be sheltered by your Estate Tax Exclusions (beware the trap of the Unlimited Marital Deduction), you may conclude that you are not a candidate for the New Estate Planning. Now, however, assume that the value of your assets increases at an average annual rate of 8%. Divide 72 by 8, and you have just calculated that in 9 years you will have combined estates of $6,000,000. The estate tax generated by such an estate could be as much as $2,000,000. If you and your spouse live until age 76, the Rule of 72 tells us that your combined estates could exceed $48,000,000!

True, for any number of reasons, including adjustment for inflation, in today's dollars the actual growth in assets experienced by our 40-year old couple may be significantly less than $45,000,000. By the same token, it may be equally plausible to assume that their taxable estates will be significantly increased after age 40, by savings, inheritance, and/or an average rate of growth exceeding 8%.

The Rule of 72 is not a crystal ball. However, the power of compounding reflected in the Rule forcefully reminds us that many readers of *Beyond Death & Taxes* will eventually find themselves, or family, friends and colleagues, face to face with a "significant" estate tax problem. By planning sooner rather than later, Total Wealth Control can harness the Rule of 72 to great advantage.

Let us suppose that a few paragraphs ago you did not have a vision of an alternative for your estate tax dollars. Please close your eyes and imagine how the federal and state governments will spend those dollars... My personal favorite is interest on the national debt, which gobbles up 14¢ out of every tax dollar.

Now back to reality.

➤ Do you prefer to be an involuntary philanthropist? If not, please read on.

➤ Are your tax dollars destined to be quickly spent and forgotten because you were not aware of all your planning options? If so, it is not too late — this book is for you and your family.

➤ Are your **parents** scheduled to be involuntary philanthropists? Reading this book may help you to show them alternatives.

➤ Do you represent a **charitable organization** whose donors are subject to estate taxes? If so, this book can help you to motivate many of these donors to provide your organization with new support — both before and after their deaths.

➤ Are you looking for new sources of support for your charity? This book can help you find people who have never dreamed they could help you.

➤ Do you advise clients who are resigned to the conventional certainty of death and taxes? If so, imagine their satisfaction when you show them how they can take control.

➤ Have you been searching for planning tools that you can use to build a team of advisors who are committed to helping clients gain control over all of their wealth? If so, consider this book to be your tool box.

Effective planning evolves over a lifetime, across generations. It begins today with you.

You may not be willing or able to put an entire Zero Estate Tax Plan in place today, or next month, but you are entitled to know what options are available to you and how you can begin to create those options.

A WORD ABOUT FORMAT AND JABBERWOCKY

Are you sitting in your favorite chair at home, in a **quiet oasis** in your schedule? Or are you perhaps on an airplane, with a couple of tranquil hours to fill? Good — you are poised to take full advantage of this book.

Two more suggestions: have a pen and a supply of those ubiquitous yellow stickers at hand.

Perhaps you already noticed the wide margins. The open space is your invitation to react and connect with the content. Have a question about a point? Take your pen and put a big "?" by that point. You might even add: "Call my Advisor about this — **tomorrow**." If you read something that surprises or even amazes you, put a "!!" beside it. Use the yellow stickers to mark key passages. By the time you finish reading, your book may be festooned with colorful stickers. *Beyond Death & Taxes* may not be a CD-ROM, but you and your imagination can make reading it a very interactive experience.

* * *

This book can provide you with general planning concepts and specific planning techniques — new answers to old questions. It cannot provide you with an exact blueprint for your own situation. In fact, one theme of *Beyond Death & Taxes* is **that there is no single right answer.** There are, however, **CHOICES**, to be made by you, your family and your advisors.

Although few specific dates are mentioned, please keep in mind that all of the basic planning concepts discussed in this book are available today. Having said that, as you move to implement a particular strategy, always remember that the law is constantly shifting. We will be seeing examples of these tides and currents, to help make the point that there are very few bright lines in the sea of planning.

As in all disciplines there are certain key terms to be learned and applied. You are about to encounter some rather exotic nomenclature. Although we furnish definitions, explanations, examples, graphics and a Glossary, there is bound to be a certain amount of Alice in Wonderland confusion as to the exact meaning of terms. Please, do not despair! In fact, I suggest that you read from beginning to end in a single flow, with as few intermissions as possible. In this way you will see the panorama of possibilities, rather than a plethora of polysyllables.

Look for three themes that weave through all of *Beyond Death & Taxes:*

➤ The powerful paradox of **control:** less <u>ownership</u> often means more control.

➤ Bringing the extended **family** closer together, through the generations.

➤ Connecting family members with **Community,** making a difference in the world beyond the family, while the family maintains control of the resources earmarked for the Community.

*   *   *

To learn more about your choices we will share the experience of the Roberts family: the parents, Charles and Amelia, and their children, Neil and Sally. The story of the Roberts family and their planning odyssey is told in flashbacks, from the starting point of Amelia Roberts at age 80.

The Roberts family is a composite of dozens of families. Their planning issues will be familiar to you.

In the end, the end is not important. The process of choosing is important. Your choices will give the ultimate meaning to old questions, new answers.

PROLOGUE

Amelia Roberts could hear the hum of voices in the next room. Amelia lay listening, her eyes closed on a warm May morning in her 80th year.

Amelia could hear the voices of her son, Neil, and her daughter, Sally. She could also distinguish the familiar tones of her lawyer, her accountant, her financial advisor, her insurance agent, and the director of The Water Wheel Society — family friends really, after so many years of counsel.

Outside her open window, Amelia could hear the sounds of grandchildren and great grandchildren, playing in the yard.

What were all these people doing gathered around her? For a moment Amelia was going to ask her husband, Charles. He must be awake by now, she thought, but then she remembered. Charles was gone. He had died several years earlier. Amelia looked at his picture on the dresser and closed her eyes again.

The voices were there because Amelia had invited them. For some time now she had not felt well. There was no specific medical problem, just the steady erosion of the years.

Amelia's doctor said her general health was actually remarkable, considering her age.

Considering her age. That was why Amelia had asked her family and her planning advisors to come to her home this May morning, continuing a lifelong process in which Amelia had tried to give careful consideration to all of the important decisions in her life. What were her planning choices? How should she plan for her priorities? How should she adjust her priorities, maintain her options?

Amelia and Charles had always believed in consulting— with each other, and with their children, from the time they were young adults. They also consulted experts, advisors and friends. Amelia and Charles always made the final decisions, and then, after more consulting, they made them again.

The ticking of the clock opened Amelia's eyes. Ten o'clock. The time she had set for this meeting to review her estate planning. Was everything in order? It was time to rise and join the others in the next room.

Amelia hadn't meant to sleep so late. She hated to keep people waiting. She thought of one of her favorite sayings: "Life is what happens while you are making plans."

Suddenly Amelia's room became very still except for the spring breeze murmuring through the curtains.

1 GOALS AND PRIORITIES

Without a clear understanding of your goals and priorities, even the use of the most sophisticated estate planning techniques will be an artificial exercise, solutions in search of a problem.

* * *

As he waited for Amelia in her living room, Frank Jones, the Roberts' family attorney for over twenty years, reflected on the array of goals that Amelia and Charles Roberts had charted for themselves. Do the Roberts' goals sound familiar?

➤ Maintain our standard of living

➤ Give our children and grandchildren a good start in life

➤ Provide funds and structure for our retirement

➤ Provide my surviving spouse and other family members with financial security

➤ Provide my surviving spouse with control over assets

➤ Maximize the value of our business interests

➤ Minimize our taxes

➤ Provide adequate cash (liquidity) to pay estate taxes

➤ Protect assets from potential creditors

These planning goals were shared by a wide range of Frank's clients. By themselves they did not really provide much guidance in shaping planning choices, but Frank had found them helpful in the creation of a framework for evaluating particular planning techniques.

* * *

Charles and Amelia Roberts also had more specific planning goals.

By the age of 60, Charles Roberts had successfully steered his company, Roberts Electronics, Inc., through several stages of challenge and growth. Now he felt a growing need to be less consumed by his business. He wanted more time with Amelia and the rest of his family. He realized that he had been so absorbed in building his business that he had spent very little time formulating his exit from the business. Perhaps he had simply been avoiding a very difficult subject.

One thing Charles knew for certain: he did not want to "retire." Not if "retire" meant no more than monitoring his orchids and investments, the occasional family visit or travel, frequent rounds of golf or sets of tennis. Although all of these activities were very important and satisfying in their own right, they were not enough. Charles had been a force all of his adult life. He still felt full of force. For him, "retirement" meant re-directing his energy and talent. But where?

Charles went to his study and quietly closed the door. With his favorite Bach cello composition on the sound system, he settled into his armchair and gazed out the window at the swirling flakes of the winter's first snow. Perhaps now, in tranquillity and repose, he would hear a voice from the future that would help him unravel the mystery of his "retirement." The flakes began to form an exquisite pattern on the pane. Charles listened, but there was no voice to be heard. He didn't have a clue.

* * *

Through the years Charles and Amelia had accumulated a substantial portfolio of securities. With the assistance of Fred Herman, their financial advisor, the Roberts owned several stocks that had greatly appreciated over their original cost.

The Roberts had also acquired 100 acres of beautiful land in the Blue Mountains, where they had built a vacation home, the center of many of the family's most memorable times together.

In addition to caring for the children and making many

of the business decisions with Charles, Amelia had also developed a number of charitable interests and activities.

* * *

These concerns and values generated several more specific planning goals for the Roberts:
- ➤ A plan for the next stage of their lives
- ➤ Diversification of their securities portfolio, to reduce risk and to increase income as retirement years approached (ideally these goals would be achieved with a minimum of tax cost)
- ➤ Achieving a higher degree of certainty as to the amount of inheritance that the children and other heirs would receive
- ➤ Creation of arrangements that would involve the children in financial planning and management, with the guidance of Charles and Amelia
- ➤ Preservation of the Blue Mountain property for the continuing use and enjoyment of the children and grandchildren
- ➤ Providing personal participation and financial support for charitable activities in their community

The Roberts family and their advisors realized that these goals were not entirely compatible. Some trade-offs would be required. **For example, as a general rule, the more ownership you have over assets, the more taxes you will pay — if creditors don't take the assets first.**

Striking a balance among the Roberts' goals required a

clear but flexible set of priorities. Their method was to create and preserve the maximum number of options, while taking the least drastic irrevocable action.

* * *

If you have a clear vision of your priorities, you have already made critical progress in your planning. However, as the Roberts came to learn, before you can proceed with specific planning techniques your priorities must take into account the priorities of another very influential family member: Uncle Sam.

2 KEY TAX CONCEPTS

Identifying your goals and setting your priorities will be very effective if you take your family, financial and personal situation into account. However, before you can translate goals and priorities into a planning program, you must reckon with other powerful forces.

* * *

Sitting in the Roberts' living room, their accountant, Susan Anderson, listened to the birds singing their spring songs. Each song undoubtedly had a clear meaning — at least for the birds. Susan felt a sense of satisfaction as she remembered how the Roberts had gradually become more comfortable in speaking the esoteric language of the tax code.

Here are several of the fundamental tax rules that had a major impact upon the Roberts' planning:

➤ You may transfer a total of **$1,500,000** at the time of your death, with no federal estate tax: **THE ESTATE TAX EXCLUSION.** The exclusion may increase to $3,500,000 by 2009.

➤ The estate tax is scheduled to disappear 2010, then reappear in 2011: stay tuned for changes in the law.

➤ You may transfer a total of $1,000,000 during your lifetime, with no federal gift tax: **THE GIFT TAX EXCLUSION**

➤ Property transferred to your spouse, either during lifetime or upon death, will generally qualify for the federal **UNLIMITED MARITAL DEDUCTION** — no tax will be due

➤ You may make an annual gift of up to **$11,000** to an unlimited number of other persons—without reducing your Estate Tax Exclusion or your Gift Tax Exclusion: **THE ANNUAL EXCLUSION GIFT**, hereinafter simply referred to as the **ANNUAL GIFT**

➤ In addition to Annual Gifts, you can pay tuitions and medical expenses—without reducing your Gift Tax Exclusion

➤ Federal gift and estate tax rates are high: **48%** is the top federal bracket

➤ State death taxes range up to **16%**

➤ For most assets that you have owned for at least one year, **CAPITAL GAINS TAX** rate is **15%**

➤ You will pay no capital gain tax on the first $250,000 of gain from the vale of your principal residence

➤ The income tax rate on qualified dividends is **15%**, compared to a top rate of **35%** for interest

➤ Lifetime gifts to qualified charitable organizations may be eligible for income tax deductions

➤ Your retirement plan benefits may be ravaged by a daunting array of income and transfer taxes

➤ When a grandparent transfers property directly to or for the benefit of a grandchild, or younger heir, a **48% GENERATION-SKIPPING TRANSFER**

TAX (GST)— will apply, after a GST Exemption of $1,500,000

➤ <u>Generally</u> speaking, if you are married, then for tax purposes it will be to your advantage to equalize the size of your estates

➤ If you are married, you and your spouse may elect to <u>split</u> your gifts, for purposes of Annual Gifts, the Gift Tax Exclusion, and the GST Exemption. **Gift-Splitting** can greatly facilitate your use of these powerful planning tools.

➤ Upon your death, any property transferred to qualified charitable organizations will be eligible for an unlimited deduction—**THE ESTATE TAX CHARITABLE DEDUCTION**

If you are married, full use of your Estate Tax Exclusion and the Unlimited Marital Deduction should generally result in no federal tax on the death of the first spouse. You gain the benefit of the Unlimited Marital Deduction through the use of special **Marital Trusts** created by the first spouse to die, for the benefit of the surviving spouse.

Warning: In order to take advantage of the Estate Tax Exclusion in <u>both</u> spouses' estates, you must do <u>two</u> things: (1) have your attorney draft Wills and Trusts that force the use of the Estate Tax Exclusion when the first spouse dies, and (2) deploy your asset ownership so that the first spouse to die will have assets in his or her estate at least equal to the current Estate Tax Exclusion. *Application of these basic planning techniques could save you and your family more than $750,000 in taxes.*

If you are not sure whether your plans—or your parents' plans—meet these requirements, take your pen and put a big star in the margin next to this paragraph. Make a note to call your attorney—or your parents—just as soon as you finish *Beyond Death & Taxes*. With that one call you may be able to reap a handsome return on your investment in this book.

* * *

Susan thought of the enormous effort she and her clients devoted every year toward the goal of reducing income taxes. She certainly appreciated the handsome fees this work produced, but she was struck by the relative lack of client time and resources directed toward the greatest tax of them all: the estate tax, which in one blow could take more than half of everything a family had struggled to build over a lifetime, and cripple or destroy the family business.

Dave Ryan, the Roberts' insurance agent, knew these tax realities well. He had been instrumental in helping the Roberts avoid many of the most devastating tax consequences through the use of the **Irrevocable Life Insurance Trust**, sometimes called the **Personal Capital Trust**.

The structure and operation of the Irrevocable Life Insurance Trust will be discussed in detail in Chapter 4. For now, simply keep in mind that this type of trust is irrevocable: once you have signed the document that creates the trust, the terms of the trust generally cannot be changed or revoked. Although a well-drafted trust will have flexibility to meet changing circumstances, the creation of an irrevocable trust does result in some loss of ownership rights. In return, you and your family may harvest enormous tax and other benefits.

The Irrevocable Life Insurance Trust illustrates one of the cardinal principles of the New Estate Planning: by modifying the formal ownership of your assets, you and your family may achieve much greater control over the assets. **Less ownership, more benefits**.

To understand this paradox, we can think in terms of "good" control and "bad" control. The "bad" or undesirable forms of control are seductive but deceptive, because in the long run, these forms of *apparent* control actually expose your family assets to a high risk of confiscation by taxes and/or creditors. Conversely, "good" control involves the engineering of arrangements that emphasize the benefits of limited but practical influence, rather than outright, formal, legal ownership of assets.

Under current law, the basic tax benefit of a properly-drafted Irrevocable Life Insurance Trust is clear: insurance on your life originally acquired by such a Trust will not be included in your taxable estate, or in the estate of your spouse.

Example: your estate is in the 48% estate tax bracket. You purchase and own a $1,000,000 policy on your life. When you pass away, Uncle Sam may end up with $480,000, with up to $160,000 in state death tax. Now suppose the insurance were acquired and held by an Irrevocable Life Insurance Trust: there would be no estate tax! Zero!

To be sure, such a Trust offers many other advantages, including the opportunity to build cash value inside an insurance policy without being subject to any income tax. Furthermore, when the insurance proceeds are paid to the Trust upon the death of the insured, no income tax is due.

One other fundamental set of tax rules came to play a very important role in the Roberts' planning: the **Generation-Skipping Transfer Tax.**

To understand these rules, let us first imagine a world in which there were no Generation-Skipping Tax. In such a world it would be possible to transfer substantial wealth to an Irrevocable Trust, either by means of life insurance proceeds, or by gifts of other property. Imagine that those funds were provided by "Grandparent." She might have to pay a gift or estate tax when she transferred these funds to the Trust in the first place. However, once the funds were inside the trust, they could be invested and eventually distributed to children, grandchildren, or even great grandchildren—with no additional gift or estate tax. The reason: under a properly-drafted Trust, none of the beneficiaries of the Trust would have enough ownership of the trust property to trigger further tax.

Until 1986 there was no Generation-Skipping Transfer Tax. Families with substantial estates often created generation-skipping trusts to shelter their wealth from several cycles of tax. Each generation could enjoy the income, then pass along the principal to the next generation, unscathed by estate tax.

In 1986 Congress put an end to unlimited generation skipping. In basic terms, a generation-skipping transfer tax—at the top estate tax rate— was imposed on every transfer of property to a person who was two generations or more younger than the original transferor. Example: Grandparent, the original transferor, transfers $1,000,000 to Grandchild. A generation-skipping tax is due, in the amount of $480,000. This tax is in addition to gift tax!

In creating the generation-skipping tax, Congress did allow one very important exception. You can transfer up to $1,500,000 to or for the benefit of a grandchild, or even younger generations—with no generation-skipping transfer tax. Your **GST Exemption** can be put to very powerful use inside an **Irrevocable Trust**.

* * *

Frank Jones had also helped clients to extend the life of Irrevocable Trusts that were **grandfathered** (exempted) from the generation-skipping tax, because the Trusts had been created before the effective date of the tax: September

25, 1985. In one such case, Robert Redwood had created a Revocable Trust in 1955. At the time of his death in 1975, the Redwood Trust became irrevocable. At his death, Robert had several grandchildren, the youngest of whom was Fern, age 1. The principal asset of the Redwood Trust was the controlling stock of the family business, worth $3,000,000 in 1975. By the time Robert's son, Randall Redwood, came to see Frank, the stock was worth $12,000,000. Examining the Redwood Trust instrument, Frank found that Randall had a **testamentary limited power of appointment** over the Trust, which allowed Randall, upon his death, to direct the Trust assets to a revocable **Continuation Trust**, for the benefit of Randall's children, Randall's other issue, and the spouses of Randall's issue. The new Trust would have the tax, asset protection and control features that you will see in Chapter 4.

Frank calculated that the Continuation Trust could reasonably be expected to last for 100 years. During that time it would support several generations of the Redwood descendants—with no transfer tax on the Trust assets being due during all that time.

If you think about $12,000,000, and 100 years, and the Rule of 72, you will understand why Randall Redwood was a happy client on the day he signed the Continuation Trust and a **Codicil** (amendment) to his Will exercising the limited power of appointment.

You will also understand why Frank always made a point

of carefully checking all older Trusts to see if there were other grandfathering opportunities.

Are you, your parents, or anyone else in your family the beneficiary of a trust that became irrevocable before September 25, 1985? If that is so, or if you are not certain, put a sticker in the margin and be sure to call your attorney—right after you finish reading this book. *That sticker could be worth a small (or large) fortune for you and your family.*

* * *

Opportunities like the Continuation Trust occur frequently, because the New Estate Planning expands your planning horizons beyond the **nuclear family**, to embrace parents, grandparents, aunts, uncles, siblings, children, and grandchildren. The **extended family**, once endangered as families dispersed geographically, has been reconstituted in the New Estate Planning as a powerful source of human and financial connection. Some family members may be out of sight, but in the era of E-mail, the cybernetic family may easily conquer the miles.

* * *

We will see exactly how an **Irrevocable Trust** can work as we learn more about the tools used to build the Roberts' plan, but first we will discover how the Roberts designed their blueprint.

3 THE BASIC STRATEGIES OF TOTAL WEALTH CONTROL

The Roberts and their advisors had reached a crossroads. By employing all of the advanced techniques available for minimizing estate taxes, they believed that they had created a "state of the art" plan— but something was missing. To be exact, over $4,000,000 was missing.

With combined assets of $10,000,000, the Roberts were still faced with a projected federal and state estate tax bill of over $4,000,000. When they were told by previous advisors "not to worry— there will be enough cash to pay the estate tax bill," the Roberts felt less than elated by this "good news."

The Roberts were not absolutely opposed to paying taxes. To the contrary, they realized and accepted that taxes were a form of "Community Capital." Taxes provide federal and state governments with the means to support programs intended to provide a wide range of benefits to society.

That was the conventional wisdom. Yet the Roberts were not eager to provide Community Capital in the form of more taxes. For one thing, they had already paid an enormous amount of <u>income</u> <u>tax</u>. Furthermore, the $4,000,000 slated for estate taxes represented a very substantial portion of the Roberts' investment in Community Capital.

The Roberts knew from personal experience that the government did not have a monopoly on providing community benefits. Through a number of charitable organizations, the Roberts were able to promote and support programs in their own Community and beyond that had a direct and significant impact on the lives of many people.

Given their choice, the Roberts preferred Community solutions to Community problems.

The Roberts sensed that the fundamental dilemma for them was not <u>whether</u> a substantial portion of their wealth would be used for public benefits— that was both desirable and inevitable. The real question was: who would <u>control</u> the type and form of benefits? Would it be the Roberts family, or the government?

This is the choice between involuntary philanthropy and voluntary philanthropy. **Which would you rather do: pay estate tax, or make charitable gifts, controlled by you and your family?**

If you are fully aware of your ability to chose, you are in a position to apply **Total Wealth Control** to all of your assets, including the very substantial portion that all people of wealth must allocate to Community Capital. Whether you then choose to pay Zero Estate Tax, or Maximum Estate Tax, or an amount somewhere on the spectrum between these two points, is less important than your being able to make a series of fully-informed choices.

As this realization dawned on the Roberts, Amelia was troubled by the sense that her choosing to guide the flow of her Community Capital was presumptuous— she was making the policy, instead of leaving the choice to the government and the political process.

It was Amelia's daughter, Sally, who helped her mother through this difficulty. Having been a development officer for a local university, Sally was quite familiar with the tax rules and policies that supported her institution. She pointed out to Amelia that the American people, acting through Congress, had long ago decided that sound public policy was well served by encouraging gifts to charitable organizations.

Over the years our Congress has provided many incentives for charitable gifts. This policy reflects a belief at the core of our system: government is necessary to do those things that we the people are unable to do for ourselves. In the modern era, government has a vital role, but perhaps no role is more important and productive than the creation of incentives that enable people to help themselves, their families, and their communities.

The tradition of private and public support for charitable organizations has long been a hallmark of our American system. Stewardship of our material blessings is central to our American experience. The spirit of the Community barn-raising still breathes in our collective character.

In 2002, Americans made over $240,000,000,000 in charitable gifts!

We Americans benefit greatly from the support given to charitable organizations and from the special tax rules that encourage that support. So many of our Community institutions are dependent upon and nourished by charitable gifts: universities, hospitals, museums, the performing arts, and religious organizations, to name a few.

Without private support, many if not most of these institutions would either wither for lack of funds, or else be controlled by the federal government.

From another perspective, there may be both a moral and practical imperative to invest our Community Capital wisely. The value of our "Personal Capital"—assets that we can consume for our own personal use— depends directly on our Community, which cannot be totally insulated from the rest of our society. As John Donne might have said: "No dollar is an island."

* * *

Sally was also able to explain to Amelia that the estate tax generates a very small portion of the total federal budget. Amelia's share of Community Capital posed no threat whatsoever to the solvency of the government.

The Roberts' son, Neil, participated in the family discussions about the role and importance of charitable organizations. A successful businessman in his own right, Neil had made wise use of the opportunities provided by Charles and Amelia. He shared his sister's faith in a strong charitable system, but he also brought a pragmatic orientation to the family's wealth. He asked a basic question: if his parents adopted a plan whereby they gave half of their estate to charitable organizations, was it not true that the amount of the direct inheritance for the children and grandchildren would be cut in half? Assuming a combined federal and state estate tax bracket of 50%, all the advisors had to agree the answer was "yes." However, they also agreed that the value of the inheritance might be more than doubled, through prudent planning.

The approach that emerged from these discussions was what Frank Jones, the family attorney, called **Total Wealth Control**.

The Roberts adopted these basic strategies to implement their version of Total Wealth Control:

➤ **ESTABLISH THE "MINIMUM PERSONAL CAPITAL" FOR THEIR CHILDREN AND OTHER HEIRS**

The Roberts used the term "Personal Capital" to distinguish it from Community Capital. For the Roberts, Personal Capital meant assets that their children and younger generations of heirs could actually spend for their own personal use— to buy a home, educate children, pay medical bills, and so forth.

The Roberts established a Personal Capital goal of $6,000,000.

Please note that the choice of $6,000,000 as the "minimum" target for Personal Capital was the result of a complex process that evolved over many years. It was the product of discussions not only between Amelia and Charles, but also with their children, Neil and Sally, as they moved through adulthood.

For you, the initial selection of the Minimum Personal Capital may be among the most difficult — and empowering— of all of your planning decisions. Using Total Wealth Control, you are taking a proactive position as to the optimal amount and form of inheritance that you wish to provide to your children and other heirs. You are making the allocation between Personal Capital and Community Capital, rather than simply waiting for the government to roll the dice of estate tax calculations, in which the amount of Personal Capital becomes a random event.

In his law practice, Frank Jones had encountered a very broad spectrum of thinking on the balance between Personal Capital and Community Capital. Some clients and their advisors concluded that optimal Personal Capital should consist of the maximum amount of assets that the tax system would allow parents to pass directly to their children—regardless of how much gift or estate tax was incurred in the process.

Frank had also worked with an equal if not larger number of families in which a major concern was that too much wealth would rob their heirs of motivation to work hard, and weaken their sense of responsibility to the larger Community. For these families, protection against excessive wealth was at least as important as protection against excessive taxes. These clients wished to provide their children ample assets to make a solid start in life— to educate themselves and their own children, to the full extent of their capabilities; to purchase a comfortable though not extravagant home; to establish themselves in a business, profession or career that offers a reasonable potential for personal fulfillment and a comfortable standard of living, yet still provides strong incentive to be a productive member of the Community.

Having assured that their children and other heirs would have enough assets for a solid start in life, this group of Frank's clients were keenly interested in another form of legacy for their children: *the active stewardship of material blessings that good fortune has entrusted to us*. These clients were deeply motivated to act as stewards of the Community Capital that would provide the family, both during the parents' lifetimes and after their deaths, with the opportunity to develop, express, and build family values oriented towards the larger Community. They could choose from among many arrangements for structuring this form of legacy, but Frank had observed that almost universally the legacy of Community Capital seemed to provide his clients with two very deep sources of satisfaction:

- **A bonding of the family**, both present and future generations, through the articulation and implementation of charitable activities to be served by the family's Community Capital.

- A belief that the clients were in some way going to **leave their corner of the world a little better than they found it.**

Frank realized that to some people, these values might seem nostalgic, drawn from a Norman Rockwell painting. However, as his clients became more aware of mortality, they welcomed a way to leave behind some trace of themselves— a connection to something of significance, something beyond their "bottom line."

Early in his practice, Frank had realized that it was not feasible, much less appropriate, to "judge" the way in which different families struck the balance between Personal Capital and Community Capital.

The planning goal was not to be "right" or "wrong," but to create peace of mind, based upon full knowledge of the choices.

➤ **ASSURE THE MINIMUM PERSONAL CAPITAL BY MEANS OF INSURANCE HELD IN AN IRREVOCABLE TRUST, SOMETIMES REFERRED TO AS A "WEALTH REPLACEMENT TRUST"**

None of the insurance proceeds would be taxed in either Charles' estate or Amelia's estate.

The Trust would be designed to provide Neil and Sally with separate, equal shares. Income and/or principal could be used to maintain their respective family's established standard of living, for example, to provide housing, education, and travel.

The Trust would also be designed to give Neil and Sally a great deal of control over the distribution of trust funds during their lifetimes, and then upon their deaths. At <u>their</u> deaths, none of the trust assets would be taxed in their estates. *The assets would skip a layer of tax, without having to skip a generation of benefits.*

➤ **INCREASE THE MINIMUM PERSONAL CAPITAL WITH LIFETIME GIFTS OF PROPERTY TO THE CHILDREN AND GRANDCHILDREN**

The Roberts would make use of their Gift Tax Exclusions and Annual Gifts to carry out this part of the strategy. They would also help with non-taxable payments of tuition for grandchildren.

In addition, the Roberts would use the **goodwill** from their family business, Roberts Electronics, and their own business skills, to create new businesses initially controlled by them, but owned by generation-skipping trusts for the benefit of their children and other heirs. For this invaluable transfer of intangible property, no Annual Gifts or Unified Credits would be required.

The creation of new business entities also serves the goal of **asset protection**, by minimizing the extent to which liabilities in one business could damage the value of your other businesses.

Although tax considerations loom large in the strategy of lifetime gifts, as in other areas of the New Estate Planning, tax benefits should not obscure *the very powerful human dimension of gifts*. Gifts of liquid assets, such as cash or publicly-traded stock, can bring pure and profound joy to a child struggling to buy a first home, or to start a business, or to educate her own children. Economic realities have changed dramatically for younger generations. If you are in your 50's or older, think back to what you paid for your first home, or to go to college. Even after adjusting for inflation, the cost of these and other "basic" elements of the American dream has skyrocketed.

Your lifetime gifts can make the crucial difference between decades of financial anxiety, and a life empowered by a sense of fundamental financial security.

> **PLACE A CONSERVATION EASEMENT ON THE BLUE MOUNTAIN PROPERTY, TO ASSURE THAT IT WOULD BE FOREVER PROTECTED FROM UNCONTROLLED DEVELOPMENT, AND ALSO TO REDUCE ITS VALUE FOR ESTATE TAX PURPOSES**

When Charles and Amelia both had passed away, the Wealth Replacement Trust would have sufficient funds to purchase Blue Mountain from the parents' estates, thereby making the property available for the use and enjoyment of future generations of the Roberts family— free from the cycle of crushing transfer taxes.

> **UPON THE DEATH OF CHARLES AND AMELIA, THE VALUE OF ALL PROPERTY REMAINING IN THEIR ESTATES WOULD PASS TO A CHARITABLE ORGANIZATION CREATED AND CONTROLLED BY THE ROBERTS FAMILY— THE ROBERTS FAMILY FOUNDATION**

All of the property passing to The Roberts Family Foundation would qualify for the estate tax charitable deduction— thereby eliminating all estate tax.

The Roberts Family Foundation could have an endowment of as much as $7,000,000, providing $350,000 that would be available <u>every year</u> for distribution to other charitable organizations, or for the charitable activities of the Foundation itself.

* * *

These were the basic strategies adopted by the Roberts. In the following Chapters, we will examine the specific planning tools they used to carry out their strategies.

4 THE IRREVOCABLE INSURANCE TRUST OR PERSONAL CAPITAL TRUST

Before we continue the saga of Charles and Amelia, we should pause to introduce a small but very important set of estate planning terms.

You create an **Irrevocable Trust** when you sign a special form of document prepared by your attorney. You are referred to in the document as the **Donor** or **Grantor**. The document, known as an **Agreement** or **Indenture of Trust**, specifies that persons referred to as **Trustees** will hold and distribute property for the benefit of persons designated as **beneficiaries**. If you give up the right to change the terms of the trust, such as the right to change the beneficiaries, the Trust is **irrevocable**.

An Irrevocable Trust funded with substantial assets is sometimes referred to as a **Personal Capital Trust**, since one of its primary purposes is to help assure a direct form of inheritance for children and other heirs (Personal Capital), by replacing dollars that would either be taken by the government in the form of estate taxes, or else made available to one or more charitable organizations directed by your Family (Community Capital).

An Irrevocable Trust that owns insurance on the lives of

one or more of the Grantors is often referred to as an **Irrevocable Life Insurance Trust**. The Irrevocable Life Insurance Trust is a very important, though by no means exclusive, form of **Wealth Replacement Trust**.

How did Charles and Amelia design their Wealth Replacement Trust?

The <u>first step</u> was to determine the amount of insurance desired by the Roberts. As you may remember, they had chosen $6,000,000 as the Minimum Personal Capital for their heirs. Assuming that $3,000,000 of this goal could be met by their existing assets, and sheltered from estate tax by their combined Unified Credits, that left $3,000,000 as the potential need for insurance.

Since the insurance dollars were needed not on the first death, but rather upon the death of the survivor of Charles and Amelia, the Roberts readily accepted the recommendation of their insurance agent, Dave Ryan, to use a type of insurance policy called **joint life** or **second-to-die insurance**. The death benefit would be paid when the second spouse died. By spreading the maturity of the policy over two lives, the insurance companies have more time to build up the funds to pay the death benefit. That is why the *annual premiums for one joint life policy are substantially lower than for two single life policies*.

In presenting the Roberts with numerous funding options, Dave pointed out that although the use of joint life insurance results in lower <u>annual</u> premiums, the Roberts would pay substantially more in <u>total</u> premiums, per dollar of death benefit, than if they had chosen to obtain the same amount of death benefit on just one of their lives, or separate policies on each of their lives. In this respect, the financing of insurance resembles the familiar financing of your home by means of a mortgage: the shorter the term of the mortgage, for example, 15 years compared to 30 years, the larger the potential accumulation of equity in your home. However, the Roberts had competing uses for their available cash flow, so they opted for the more gradual form of premium payments.

Next, the Roberts took **insurance physicals**, arranged by Dave. The results of these examinations, together with reports and records from their physicians, were furnished to three insurance companies selected by Dave for their financial strength and competitive premiums.

It is important for you to select a flexible range as to the amount of insurance you will be seeking <u>before</u> you proceed with the physical, because the amount of insurance may affect the extent of the physical. If you take a physical designed for a $2,000,000 policy, then later decide that you really need $4,000,000 of coverage, you may have to schedule more tests, or even have some tests done again.

About one month after the insurance physicals, Dave had firm policy offers from the three insurance companies. Dave now knew that $3,000,000 of coverage was actually available from the carriers. The policies would be split equally among the insurance companies, each of which carried the highest ratings for financial strength and policy performance. The Roberts and all of their advisors agreed that it was *wise to diversify* this major element of their estate planning.

The Roberts realized that **from an investment perspective, there is nothing magical about life insurance.** If they died after reaching their full life expectancy, they could expect the cash value of their insurance policies to have grown at an annual average rate of between 5% and 9%. Charles was confident that he could take the same dollars to be used for insurance premiums and invest them (through an Irrevocable Trust) to yield 10% or more, even after allowing for income tax (you pay no income tax on the increase in value of a life insurance policy). However, Charles also recognized that if he and Amelia were to die before their life expectancy, the rate of return on the insurance premiums could be astronomical. For example, in the "worst" case, if spouses make a payment of a single $10,000 premium and then they both die in an accident, that investment could generate a $1,000,000 death benefit (depending on their age and health when the insurance was purchased).

Charles and Amelia considered life insurance to be *an appropriate part of a balanced portfolio of investments.*

Charles and Amelia also realized that for them, <u>life insurance was the key to timing of their Total Wealth</u>

Control. As soon as the life insurance was in place, they had peace of mind in directing the Community Capital portion of their estates to the Roberts Family Foundation— because the Minimum Personal Capital for their children and other heirs was assured.

Even if Charles looked at insurance strictly as an investment— ignoring its unique feature of a large death benefit no matter how few premiums had been paid— he was very willing to accept a lower after-income tax rate of return on a fraction of the family assets in exchange for the **instant certainty** that the Roberts' entire plan for Total Wealth Control would produce the desired results, regardless of when he and Amelia actually passed away.

Having selected the amount of coverage, and the insurance companies to provide it, the Roberts next worked closely with Dave and the other advisors to decide how they would pay the premiums. The possibilities ranged from a single large payment, to a program of much lower annual payments, based upon a combination of **term** and **permanent** life insurance.

Structuring the premiums required a careful analysis of current and projected cash flow requirements. At age 60, with retirement in mind, the Roberts determined that they would like to make payments for only eight years, when Charles anticipated a drop in his earned income. At the end of eight years the dividends earned by the policies were conservatively projected to be sufficient to eliminate the need for any further premium payments.

Although this arrangement is sometimes referred to as a "**vanishing**" premium, your insurance agent would be the first to confirm that in fact the policy will always have an annual cost or premium. Under the vanish arrangement, it is anticipated that at the end of a specified number of years, the cost of the insurance will be paid from the dividends earned by the policy. If the dividends turn out to be lower than anticipated, then you will need to pay the premium for one or two or three more years. Conversely, if the actual dividends exceed projections, then the policy may become "self-supporting" earlier than you had expected. Your agent will monitor the actual performance of the dividends and keep you advised.

For the Roberts, annual payments in the amount of $100,000 also made sense from a tax perspective. The beneficiaries of the Wealth Replacement Trust would be their children, Neil and Sally, together with the six grandchildren (any other grandchildren or great-grandchildren born in the future would automatically become beneficiaries, too). By designing the Trust so that the gifts from Charles and Amelia would qualify for Annual Gifts, using **limited powers of withdrawal**, the Roberts could give as much as $176,000 a year to the Trust— without making any use of their Estate Tax Exclusions (8 beneficiaries x $11,000 per beneficiary x 2 donors = $176,000). The actual premium structure selected would leave $76,000 for other forms of

Annual Gifts to their children and grandchildren.

You may take further advantage of your Annual Gifts by including spouses of children or grandchildren as beneficiaries of your Trust. If you are concerned about divorce, or the death of a spouse, your Trust may limit eligibility of spouses to persons who are married to your heirs at the relevant time for distributions from the Trust.

If you do not have children or grandchildren, but would like your Trust to provide for other relatives, or friends, you can use the Annual Gifts techniques to fund a Trust for their benefit.

The total projected gifts for the Roberts' Personal Capital Trust also made sense in terms of the Generation-Skipping Tax. As you remember from Chapter 2, Charles and Amelia each had a $1,500,000 GST Exemption. By allocating $100,000 of their GST Exemptions to each set of Annual Gifts, *the Roberts would protect the entire death benefit of the insurance policies from any generation-skipping tax, gift or estate tax for several generations.*

The potential leverage of such an "innoculation" could be very powerful. For example, if the Roberts were to die three years after creating their Wealth Replacement Trust, by using only $300,000 of their GST Exemptions, they would have sheltered $3,000,000 of insurance proceeds from transfer tax for 100 years or more!

The long-term savings for the family could be even

greater. If Neil and Sally did not need to use any of the income or principal from the Wealth Replacement Trust during their lifetimes, the insurance proceeds could be invested and accumulated during their lifetimes. At a net growth rate of 6%, the value of the Trust would double every twelve years (the Rule of 72!). When Neil and Sally (and their spouses) died, none of this expanded wealth would be subject to tax in their estates. Instead, the full amount would be available to provide financial security for their children— and even younger generations— with no additional transfer tax. If the effective tax rate in their estates were 50%, the potential tax savings would be enormous.

Now you can see why these Trusts are also sometimes referred to as "**Dynasty Trusts**."

* * *

When Charles and Amelia had both died, and their Irrevocable Trust received the death benefit, who would control the Trust assets?

Under conventional estate planning, such Trusts would be designed to be distributed outright in equal shares to your children, say, in three stages, culminating in full distribution when each child reached age 35. Such an approach offers very valuable benefits, by avoiding estate tax when the parents die. However, the New Estate Planning recognizes that with such a design, the glass is only half full.

<u>When the children die</u>, any portion of the original death benefit still unspent or not given away would be <u>exposed to estate tax—</u> at rates up to 50%. Furthermore, during the children's lifetimes, their outright shares of the death benefits would be subject to the claims of "creditors" other than the tax collectors: divorce claims, business risks, claims for negligence, breaches of duty as a trustee or other **fiduciary**, claims arising from ownership of real estate contaminated by hazardous waste— the list of risks is long and growing. By contrast, assets that remain behind the ramparts of an Irrevocable Trust will have much greater protection from these very real risks.

Does a well-drafted trust <u>guarantee</u> absolute protection of assets? Absolutely not. As in many other areas of the law, the border between creditors' rights and asset owners' rights is constantly shifting. However, you can be absolutely certain that when you create a well-drafted Irrevocable Trust for the benefit of your children or others, you are adding value to the assets, when compared to your making outright transfers.

Please bear in mind that when we talk about <u>asset protection</u> as an integral part of Total Wealth Control, we are <u>not</u> talking about avoiding legitimate, existing claims or creditors. *We are talking about the perfectly legal right that you have to structure your affairs so as to minimize rather than maximize the risk of a substantial or even devastating loss of assets.* If all other things are equal, and Plan A offers greater asset protection than Plan B, you have every right to choose Plan A.

Some would even say that asset protection is not merely your right— it is your duty. If you own valuable assets, and family members or others are depending upon you for their financial security, they have both an interest and an expectation that you will take all reasonable steps to protect those assets. The expectation is all the more compelling if we view the family as an economic partnership, in which the individual whose name happens to be on a given asset is secondary to the overriding need to preserve the asset for the benefit of all.

* * *

When Charles and Amelia first told Neil and Sally about their intention to create an Irrevocable Generation-Skipping Trust, to be funded with joint life insurance, their children's initial reaction was very positive. The potential tax savings and asset protection for the children's Personal Capital were absolutely compelling. Yet on further reflection, Neil and Sally expressed reservations about <u>control</u>. Who would the Trustee be— The Friendly Bank? Sally and Neil knew and liked many of the Bank's current trust officers. However, they could well imagine a day when as beneficiaries they would have to ask different trust officers for distribution of income or principal. What if their trust officer exercised his/her best judgment and refused to make the requested distribution? Such a scenario made them wonder about the risk of <u>Impersonal</u> Capital.

Neil had other concerns. What if his wife were to die, or if they were to be divorced? If Neil were to remarry, how could he assure that upon his death the Trust assets would be available for his mate of twenty or thirty or forty years?

What if a child or grandchild of Neil's were to suffer a serious illness and require a disproportionate share of the Trust assets?

What if reckless or improvident behavior revealed that a child's or grandchild's share of assets needed additional protection, or perhaps should be reduced or eliminated altogether?

Both Neil and Sally wanted the Trust to be <u>flexible</u> enough to help build family dreams— and to minimize the impact of family nightmares.

* * *

Amelia and Charles also saw important control issues. For example, the joint life policies selected for the Trust would build up substantial **cash value** during their lifetimes. What if there were another Great Depression and their children and grandchildren needed the cash— would the Trustee be able and willing to make the cash available?

Frank Jones, the family attorney, explained that the Trustee could borrow against the **cash surrender value** of the policies, and distribute the cash to or for the benefit of Neil, Sally, or their children. The Trust would have no obligation to repay the "loan," although if the loan were not repaid, the death benefit would be reduced by the amount of the loan. "But," asked Charles, "what if the Trustee refuses to take the loan or to make the requested distribution?"

After extensive discussions among Charles, Amelia, Neil, Sally, and the spouses of both Neil and Sally, Frank proposed the following provisions for the Trust:

➤ Neil and Sally would have separate, equal shares, each of which would be a separate trust for tax purposes. The separate shares would give Neil and Sally flexibility to pursue different lifestyles or investment strategies.

➤ During Charles' and Amelia's lifetimes, by unanimous consent, Neil and Sally would also have the power to remove the Trustee and appoint a successor.

➤ After Charles and Amelia both died, Neil and Sally could independently remove the Trustee of their respective Trusts, and appoint successors. Each could be the Trustee of his or her own Trust, so long as the Trust had at least one **disinterested Trustee**, who held no beneficial interest in the Trust.

➤ The Trustee's **standard of discretion** for distribution of income and principal would be the **ascertainable standard**, taken directly from the Internal Revenue Code: "health, education, maintenance and support," which is the equivalent of the beneficiaries' accustomed standard of living.

➤ Distributions under the ascertainable standard could be made in any proportion among the beneficiaries, with no mandatory distribution and no requirement of equal shares. The Trustee could even exclude a beneficiary from receiving any distribution at all.

The ascertainable standard served several key purposes:

- Upon the death of Neil and Sally, none of the assets in their respective Trusts would be subject to estate tax. If the Trust did not have an ascertainable standard, Neil and Sally's powers to remove Trustees would result in a tax disaster: the Trust assets would be taxable in their estates.

- The ascertainable standard limited the risks to which the Trust assets could be exposed. For example, if Sally wanted to start a consulting business, she could not use her Trust assets for that purpose. However, the availability of the Trust assets to maintain her standard of living could enable her to use other assets for the new business. That way, even if the business failed, she and her family would still have a bedrock of financial security.

- The ascertainable standard, coupled with the Trust's **spendthrift clause**, would provide a formidable barrier against claims of the beneficiaries' potential future creditors.

- Upon Sally's or Neil's death, their respective Trusts would automatically be divided into separate Trusts, in equal shares for their respective children. (If Sally had three children, three separate Trusts would be created. If Neil had two children, his Trust would be divided into two Trusts.)

The new Trusts would operate for the benefit of the respective child and his or her children, whenever they might be born. The ascertainable standard would govern distributions. As "Primary Beneficiary," each child (at age 35) would have the power to remove Trustees and to appoint successors.

What if Neil had no surviving children or other issue at the time of his death? His Trust would continue to be held as a Generation-Skipping Trust for the benefit of Sally and her issue, until Sally's death, when it would be divided into separate Trusts for Sally's children. The reverse would occur if Sally died without children or other issue.

All of these otherwise automatic provisions would be subject to a **testamentary limited power of appointment**, exercisable by each of Neil or Sally in their respective Wills. For example, if Sally had a grandchild with special medical needs, she could exercise her power to create a separate Trust for the grandchild, with whatever share of the assets and on whatever terms seemed appropriate to her.

Neil could exercise his limited power to provide a Trust for the benefit of a new wife, should he ever remarry. These and a myriad of other uses of the limited power of appointment could be created and modified over the entire span of Neil's and Sally's lifetimes.

The existence of the limited power of appointment, whether or not it was ever exercised, would not cause any of the Trust property to be included in Sally's or Neil's estates.

If flexibility is one of your planning priorities, why would you ever create an Irrevocable Trust that did not have some form of limited power of appointment?

* * *

With Frank's proposed design, all of the adults in the Roberts family felt comfortable that the potential tax savings and asset protection of the Irrevocable Trust would not sacrifice the desired level of control. Once again, the Trust illustrated the powerful paradox of strategic reductions in the formalities of ownership that actually result in more benefits for the family.

* * *

At Frank's suggestion, Neil and Sally each had an attorney of their own choosing give them a second opinion on the proposed Trust. With minor but helpful revisions, the attorneys endorsed the design. For a reasonable additional legal fee, Neil and Sally— and their spouses— multiplied their satisfaction with the Trust.

Frank welcomed the participation of the other attorneys, because he was keenly aware of actual or potential **conflicts of interest** among the various family members. Each member of the family was entitled to scrutinize a proposed course of action from the perspective of his or her own individual interests. Although the involvement of other attorneys precluded the "efficiency" of conventional planning, in which the Patriarch or Matriarch makes all of the decisions, Frank had no doubt that the inclusionary approach ultimately resulted in a much better plan, supported by a much stronger consensus. He had seen too many situations in which the myth of family harmony turned into a legal war in which only the lawyers emerged victorious. By involving other attorneys in the planning process, the risk of such debacles could be lowered, if not altogether eliminated.

The second opinion technique became an integral part of Neil's and Sally's participation in the Roberts planning process.

* * *

Working with the Roberts and their other advisors, Dave Ryan had helped to design a series of Irrevocable Trusts that were funded with insurance on Charles' life.

At first, consistent with conventional estate planning, the primary purpose of these Trusts was to help create financial security for Amelia and the children, and to provide cash to help maintain the family business, Roberts Electronics. Later, policies were designed primarily to provide funds to pay the very large estate tax that would be due after both Charles and Amelia had died.

These arrangements had provided the Roberts with great

peace of mind—up to a certain point. Over time, however, Dave and the other advisors, including Frank Jones, the family attorney, had realized that something more was needed. Joint life insurance was the next stage in their evolution towards Total Wealth Control.

* * *

Please see Graphic I at the end of this Chapter for an illustration of a Wealth Replacement Trust, funded with joint life insurance.

* * *

How will you pay for life insurance?

Charles and Amelia were fortunate in being able to pay for their insurance program with currently available income. However, you may have other important options for funding your Personal Capital Trust.

One option would be the use of a **Charitable Remainder Trust**, to generate income tax savings and a stream of dollars to help you make gifts to the Personal Capital Trust. Please see Chapter 5 for more information.

A second possibility could be the use of your **retirement plan benefits**. The Roberts' advisors were well aware that in large estates, significant retirement plan benefits are "hollow dollars" because they will be subject to several layers of tax. Upon the death of your surviving spouse, your retirement plan benefits may be subject to estate tax at rates of 50% or more. When the retirement plan benefits are paid to your children, the benefits would be taxable as ordinary income— at a combined federal and state income tax rate that could exceed 45%. Finally, the few dollars that survive this tax gauntlet will be subject once again to estate tax when your children pass away— decreasing the funds available for your grandchildren by another 50%.

When all is said and done, for every dollar in your retirement plan, your grandchildren could receive less than fifteen cents.

Instead of the disappearing dollar scenario just described, suppose you withdrew enough money from your retirement plan to enable you to pay income tax on the withdrawn amount and then to make gifts to a Personal Capital Trust. The Trust owns life insurance on the lives of you and your spouse. By using your retirement plan dollars this way, you avoid several layers of tax. The number of dollars could expand dramatically over the lives of your children and grandchildren.

We will learn more about maximizing your retirement plan benefits in Chapter 8.

* * *

Waiting for Amelia to appear on that morning in May,

Frank Jones glanced across the room at Dave Ryan, who was regaling Susan Anderson with the latest of his anecdotes. How many times in their twenty years of working together had Frank seen Dave use his story-telling talent to set people at ease, often by subtly spinning a yarn that illustrated an otherwise dry and obscure point of insurance lore. Dave was a born salesman, in the best sense of the term. He liked people, he liked working with people, and he had a useful service to provide to clients and to his professional colleagues.

A good insurance agent is a professional, just like other professionals. He or she may be selling a product, but the product should be bought only after a thorough analysis of numerous factors. For example:

➤ What is the <u>perceived</u> problem that your life insurance is supposed to help solve?

➤ Will insurance <u>actually</u> help to solve the problem?

➤ What is your actual health? Only through insurance underwriting can this be accurately determined. Without underwriting, the use of insurance "quotes" can be highly misleading, causing much time to be lost— or perhaps the loss of a frustrated client.

➤ What dollars are available for insurance?

➤ Could you find more dollars for insurance in overlooked resources, such as a Charitable Remainder Trust and/or retirement plan benefits?

➤ When would you like to finish paying premiums?

➤ Would you like the death benefit to increase over

time, providing a hedge against inflation?

➤ Will any insurance be needed on the death of the first spouse?

➤ Would you be interested in managing some portion of the investment of your premiums, through **variable life insurance**?

➤ Are the projected premiums based upon hypothetical or actual current dividends of the insurance companies? What is the trend of the dividends? How will the proposed policies perform if the actual dividends turn out to be 6%, instead of the projected 8%?

➤ What is the appropriate blend of term insurance, whole life, or universal life?

➤ What is the financial strength of the insurance company involved? Should more than one carrier be considered?

➤ In the case of joint life insurance, when the first spouse dies, would the clients like the policy to be self-supporting, with no more premiums required?

In many if not most situations where Frank and Dave had worked together, the melding of these and other factors had resulted in an insurance program <u>designed to fit the available cash flow</u>. Of course, a large part of the challenge and satisfaction often lies in discovering that by decreasing certain expenses (such as income taxes), and/or by increasing income, you may very well <u>increase the available cash flow</u>, and thereby generate the dollars required to maintain the desired amount of insurance. All this must be done with no sacrifice in your standard of living.

The team of advisors also used software programs to project clients' cash flows throughout their life expectancies. Although such projections obviously could not be guaranteed, they did help clients with their peace of mind.

* * *

We will see in Chapter 8 how the Irrevocable Life Insurance Trust became part of the solution to Charles Roberts' dilemma about "retirement."

* * *

Summing up, Irrevocable Life Insurance Trusts may offer you many advantages:
➤ These Trusts are among the most powerful of all planning devices.
➤ These Trusts can be designed so that surviving spouses, children, and other heirs have a high degree of flexibility and control over their separate portions of the Trust.
➤ Life insurance can provide liquidity that may be critical for preservation of important family lands, a family business, an art collection or other irreplaceable assets.

With so many advantages, well may you wonder how

long the benefits of Irrevocable Life Insurance Trusts will be available. It is certainly true that Congress could remove some or all of the benefits of these Trusts, at any time, but it would be unusual and unlikely for Congress to apply any major changes in the law retroactively. If you create and fund such a Trust, it would most likely be exempted from any changes in the law.

Even in the "worst case," if Irrevocable Life Insurance Trusts became fully taxable, they would still have *the unique advantage of providing an immediate multiple of your investment, in the event of your untimely death.* They would also provide substantial asset protection benefits.

Is insurance essential for your Total Wealth Control? Absolutely not! Your family may have already created enough wealth in Irrevocable Trusts so that the Minimum Personal Capital for your children can be assured without insurance.

More importantly, effective estate planning creates **peace of mind**. If you are confident that you will live long enough to generate the desired level of Personal Capital for your children, by funding an Irrevocable Trust with Annual Gifts and/or the Unified Credit using stock or other assets, then you may not need insurance, or at least not as much of it as others would choose.

Once you know the choices and consequences, it is up to you.

PERSONAL CAPITAL TRUST
(Irrevocable Life Insurance Trust)

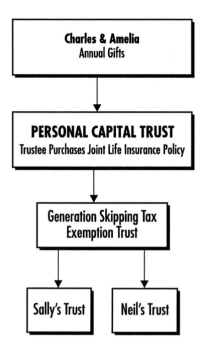

■ Allocation of generation skipping tax exemption to Annual Gifts can dramatically leverage potential tax savings

■ Separate Trusts for Sally, Neil

■ Sally and Neil have the power to remove Trustee

■ Income and principal may be distributed among Sally and Neil and their children

■ At death, Sally and Neil can direct Trust assets by means of a limited power of appointment

GRAPHIC 1

5 THE CHARITABLE REMAINDER TRUST

Across the living room from Frank Jones, Fred Herman, the Roberts' financial advisor, was studying the large globe that stood in one corner of the room. The globe reflected Charles' and Amelia's fascination with explorers. Using an ingenious system of colored lights, the globe traced the route of Columbus, Magellan, Perry and numerous others whose voyages had brought the world closer together.

As he peered closely at the flickering red pulse of Tierra del Fuego, Fred recalled a crisis in his long association with the Roberts. The investment program he had helped to create had been so successful that, as Amelia had put it, the Roberts had become *hostages of their own success*. The thought of paying the heavy capital gains tax that would have been triggered by liquidating the most highly appreciated investments in their portfolio kept them from making major changes. The Roberts were increasingly worried about the risk of holding on to these stocks— but they felt locked into the investments. Prudence and common sense were at the mercy of the tax code.

Fred had been searching for a way to unlock the appreciation in the Roberts' portfolio— without the sacrifice of the capital gains tax. It was time to reap the benefits of success, to spread and lower the investment risk, and also to increase the cash flow from these low-yield securities.

Among other things, the additional cash flow would help to support the insurance program taking shape under Dave Ryan's supervision. It would also enable Amelia to increase the level of her current charitable gifts.

Susan Anderson, the family accountant, knew that the Roberts could use another income tax deduction. Susan did not wait until April 15 to seek solutions to last year's tax problems. She had given Fred a call to see if he had any suggestions, and to see if he had heard about something with the exotic name of "Charitable Remainder Trust."

* * *

As Susan Anderson was approaching the Charitable Remainder Trust, Fred Herman, the Roberts' financial advisor, was making his own independent discovery of this powerful planning tool.

At a training seminar sponsored by his company, he was introduced to the Charitable Remainder Trust. The speaker first gave Fred and his colleagues a quiz. How many of their wealthy clients were actively involved with charitable organizations? Fred knew from his periodic review of income tax returns that many of his clients gave substantial cash gifts to charities. He was also aware that several clients were on the Boards of charitable organizations, often mixing altruistic commitment with business networking. Based on this information, Fred had estimated that perhaps 25% of his clients had a significant level of active involvement with charitable organizations. Fred's seminar colleagues had somewhat lower estimates. "In fact," boomed the speaker, "research indicates that more than 50% of wealthy individuals pursue significant charitable activities!" Fred stirred his coffee. Interesting, but where was the bottom line?

Fred's attention drifted from the speaker to the Roberts. By coincidence, Amelia Roberts was active in charitable works. However, Fred was focused on helping the Roberts escape from one of his investment triumphs: Octopus Industries, a conglomerate of maritime businesses. Octopus had been a hunch for Fred, who had recommended it to a small circle of his best clients. When Octopus struck oil in the Sea of China, the stock took off. Eventually the price settled at around $100 per share, ten times what Charles and Amelia had paid. Now, however, the triumph was turning into a trap.

Charles and Amelia had always tried to follow an investment philosophy of **diversification**, no matter how successful a specific stock had been. They wanted Fred to sell most of Octopus— on one condition: no capital gains tax! Charles informed Fred that he had paid enough capital gains tax, and he was not going to pay any more, at least not in the magnitude that would be triggered by a sale of the Octopus stock.

Fred knew that Charles was not kidding. He also knew that Charles expected Fred to find a way out of the capital gains maze. Charles was not the only client who expected Fred to extricate him from a successful investment. Success was turning ominous.

Fred made diligent inquires, but he was stumped. Since the repeal of favorable tax treatment for tax shelters, his job had become much more difficult. No longer could he conveniently help clients generate a large tax loss at the end of the year, thereby offsetting capital gains. Where was Houdini when Fred needed him?

As the speaker droned on about "Charitable Remainder Trusts," Fred surreptitiously checked the stock reports in his newspaper. Octopus was down 2. Charles Roberts and his other Octopus clients were probably on the phone right now, leaving anxious or adamant messages. Fred rose to slip away from the seminar when he heard the speaker exclaim, "With a Charitable Remainder Trust, you can sell highly appreciated stock and have no capital gains tax!" Fred felt a surge of adrenaline, and quickly sat down.

* * *

Frank Jones had come upon the Charitable Remainder

Trust from a different angle altogether. As the Roberts' family attorney, he knew that as Charles approached age 60, the complex issues entangled in the word "retirement" were pre-occupying Charles. What would happen to Roberts Electronics and all of the faithful employees who worked there? Would either or both of the Roberts' children, Sally and Neil, become involved in running the Company? If Amelia survived Charles, would she want to have primary responsibility for managing the Company?

Not the least of Charles' concerns was one that he found especially vexing, since it forced him to think of himself and his interests, to look inward: <u>once he had retired from the Company, what would he do</u>?

Amelia was well aware of Charles' struggles with retirement issues. As always, she was sympathetic, supportive and full of ideas. Many of those ideas involved one form or another of charitable enterprise.

Charles was receptive to Amelia's ideas, albeit with reservations. Already he was involved with some charitable groups, but he felt more and more constrained by their single purpose and elaborate structure. He could not see pouring the next ten or even twenty years of his life into being one more cog in someone else's operation, no matter how worthy or effective that organization might be. Being honest with himself, he freely admitted that *having a high degree of control was extremely important to him.*

One of Charles' business friends had recently given him

some literature from an organization called The Water Wheel Society. The literature included a copy of a book called *Beyond Death & Taxes*. Given his own entrepreneurial experience, the orientation of Water Wheel had a strong appeal, if only Charles could support that kind of activity with a high degree of control. In the literature he saw the name "Vera Vespucci, Executive Director." One of these days he should give her a call.

Over the course of several solitary sessions in his study, the criteria for "retirement" began to crystallize in Charles' mind. After conferring with Amelia, Neil, and Sally, Charles drafted a Memorandum to Frank Jones, including these points:

➤ Maintain financial security for Charles and Amelia.

➤ If they were both interested, give Neil and Sally the opportunity to own and run the business.

➤ If only one child had an interest in running the business, make it feasible for that to happen, while providing equivalent economic benefits to the other child. Could life insurance help to equalize the benefits?

➤ If neither child wished to manage the business, give key employees, like Jim Sullivan and Marie Paderewski, the opportunity to buy the Company.

➤ Create an arrangement that would allow Charles the freedom to set his own charitable course, with Amelia, the children, and eventually the grandchildren joining him in this new philanthropic enterprise.

➤ Come up with a better term than "retirement."

Frank Jones received the Memorandum from Charles on a Friday morning in July. He had been mulling over a suggestion for Charles that seemed to speak to Charles' general concerns about retirement. The Memorandum— a familiar form of dialogue with Charles when he and Frank were wrestling with a major decision— was the catalyst for revealing his suggestion: the Charitable Remainder Trust.

* * *

At this point and from several directions, the **Charitable Remainder Trust** made its appearance in the Roberts' planning.

You can think of the Charitable Remainder Trust as the violin of planning instruments— with proper tuning, you have a Stradivarius.

From their advisors, the Roberts learned about several potential benefits offered by a Charitable Remainder Trust:

➤ They could diversify their investments— <u>without paying capital gains tax</u>.

➤ They could double or even triple their income — <u>without paying capital gains tax</u>.

➤ Their Charitable Remainder Trust would not pay any income tax on interest, dividends or capital gains generated by its investments.

➤ They could be entitled to a significant income tax deduction for their gift to the Charitable Remainder

Trust.

➤ They could use the cash flow generated by the Charitable Remainder Trust for any number of purposes— including a program of annual gifts to a Wealth Replacement Trust, and increased contributions to charitable organizations.

➤ As Trustees, they could control investment strategy. They could hire and replace the financial advisor.

How did the Roberts' Charitable Remainder Trust work?

The Roberts transferred $1,000,000 worth of publicly-traded Octopus stock with a $50,000 cost basis and a 1% dividend to their Charitable Remainder Trust. The Trust then sold the securities in the open market. Although a capital gain was incurred by the Trust, no tax was due— because the Trust was a charitable entity, exempt from all income tax. Instead of having to forfeit $200,000 or more to the federal and state coffers, never to be seen again, the Charitable Remainder Trust allowed the Roberts to keep each one of those dollars working for them, *for the rest of their lives*.

For the rest of their lives, the Roberts could receive quarterly distributions from their Charitable Remainder Trust.

The Roberts had several choices to make in designing their Charitable Remainder Trust, including:

➤ the amount of distributions

➤ the timing of distributions

➤ the certainty of receiving the desired amount of distributions

➤ the possibility of increasing distributions to keep pace

with inflation

➤ the risk inherent in different designs of Trust

After consulting with their advisors, the Roberts chose a **pay-out rate** that would entitle them to receive the <u>lesser</u> of actual net income generated by the Trust, or an amount equal to 8% of the value of the Trust property, calculated each year. With this **net income** type of Charitable Remainder Trust, if the Trust generated net income of 8%, the Roberts would receive all of the income.

From year to year the amount of the distribution would fluctuate, depending on the value of the Trust property and the performance of the Trust portfolio.

For example, if the value of the Trust in Year One was $1,000,000, the Roberts would be entitled to $80,000. If the value of the Trust increased to $1,200,000 at the end of Year Two, they would be entitled to $96,000. On the other hand, <u>they weighed the risk</u> that the value of the Trust could decline, say to $800,000. In that case, they would be entitled to receive only $64,000 of income, again assuming that the Trust had actual net income of 8%.

If actual net income was less than 8%, the Roberts would receive that lesser amount. If actual net income was greater than 8%, the excess would be held in the Trust, to be reinvested and potentially generate more income in future years, as a hedge against inflation.

The income distributed to the Roberts <u>would be included</u>

in their taxable income, at ordinary income rates.

In addition to the lifetime stream of income, the Roberts might have been entitled to a substantial income tax deduction. The deduction would be equal to the present value of the property that would go to a Community Foundation (see Chapter 6) or other **public charity** when both Charles and Amelia had died (the "Remainder"). This is the "Charitable" component of a Charitable Remainder Trust. When you and your spouse pass away, the Trust property does not go to your children or other heirs— at least not for their personal use. Instead, it must go to a **charitable organization**. The Trust property becomes part of your family's Community Capital.

NOTE: The calculation of your income tax deduction, and your ability to use the deduction, are subject to many variables and limitations. For example, if you increase the payout rate, you decrease the deduction. Also, if you are unable to use the entire deduction in the year of the gift, you have five more tax years to apply it against your income. If, like the Roberts, you name a Family Foundation (please see Chapter 6) as the charitable organization that will eventually receive the Remainder, or if you even allow for the possibility of naming a Family Foundation, the amount and the rate of the income tax deduction may be significantly reduced or even eliminated. This equation provides yet another illustration of the inverse relationship between "control" and benefits.

NOTE: When you transfer property to a Charitable Remainder Trust, the present value of the Remainder must equal <u>at least</u> **10%** of the value of your gift.

When all is said and done, the income tax deduction may be a significant though secondary benefit of your using a Charitable Remainder Trust. Using computer software programs, your team of advisors can analyze your tax situation and then plan with you to take maximum advantage of the available deduction, consistent with your other priorities.

Please see Graphic II at the end of this chapter for an illustration of a Charitable Remainder Trust, used in part to help fund a Personal Capital Trust.

* * *

Until this moment, you may have been thinking that a Charitable Remainder Trust was a wonderful tax-planning tool— too good to be true. Your suspicions are confirmed! If it were <u>your</u> $1,000,000, you would leave it to your children, not some impersonal charity that provides no lasting benefit to your family.

Fortunately, those are <u>obsolete answers to important concerns</u>. Instead, using the New Estate Planning, let us take a closer look at what would actually happen to $1,000,000 worth of highly-appreciated stock (or land) if you sold that property yourself rather than using a Charitable Remainder Trust. We will call this the "conventional" approach to selling such property.

First, the $1,000,000 would be reduced to approximately $800,000 after you paid the federal and state capital gains tax . Then, upon your death, the federal and state estate tax could consume 50% of that value— leaving $400,000 for your children .

Here you have another striking example of involuntary, invisible philanthropy. **You gave away 60% of the value of the property— in taxes.** Stated differently, outright ownership enabled you to achieve total outright <u>control</u> of a <u>portion</u> of the property— by giving away most of it.

The Roberts were aware of these facts. In pursuit of Total Wealth Control, they chose voluntary philanthropy by building an estate plan that included the Personal Capital Trust, funded with insurance to assure that their children would receive the desired amount of Personal Capital. For you and your family that amount might be <u>more or less</u> than your heirs would have received under the conventional estate planning.

The distributions generated by a Charitable Remainder Trust, sometimes augmented by income tax savings arising from the gifts to the Trust, will very often make it possible for you to replace the value of the property that would otherwise have passed to your children ($400,000 in the example above.) Moreover, it is often quite feasible for you to replace the <u>entire</u> value of the assets transferred to the Charitable

Remainder Trust. Furthermore, by converting that Personal Capital into assets held inside a Personal Capital Trust that takes full advantage of your GST Exemptions, you not only provide Personal Capital for your heirs, but you may also greatly reduce estate taxes on your children's estates.

Not least, in this litigious day and age, the Wealth Replacement Trust will protect assets from future creditors and predators.

* * *

The Charitable Remainder Trust played a key role in the preservation and continuity of Roberts Electronics and also in Charles' retirement planning.

First, Charles and Amelia gave a small number of shares of stock in the Company to an Irrevocable Generation-Skipping Trust whose beneficiaries were Sally, Neil and the grandchildren. Charles and Amelia then made gifts of Company stock to the Charitable Remainder Trust. Under no legal obligation, the Company then redeemed those shares from the Charitable Remainder Trust. (All other stockholders must be given the same opportunity to redeem their shares.) The cash received by the Charitable Remainder Trust was invested to provide additional income for Charles and Amelia during their lifetimes. Meanwhile, as a result of the redemption, the ownership and growth in the value of the business was gradually shifted from Charles and Amelia to the Irrevocable Generation-Skipping Trust. All of this was accomplished with no gift or other transfer tax.

Amelia and Charles designed the Irrevocable Generation-Skipping Trust so that Neil and Sally could remove the Trustees and appoint successors.

If you want to use the redemption method, but you are concerned about keeping control of the business, you can use non-voting stock for gifts to the Charitable Remainder Trust, and/or to the Irrevocable Generation-Skipping Trust.

CAUTION: If your business is currently organized as an S corporation, remember that under federal income tax laws, the income of an S corporation is taxed only once, to its stockholders. However, if you transfer stock in an S corporation to a Charitable Remainder Trust, S status will be terminated because a Charitable Remainder Trust is not one of the limited types of shareholders permitted to own "S" stock. Legislation may one day correct this rather arbitrary handicap; in the meantime, the appeal of S corporations is waning for several reasons, including the availability of **Family Limited Partnerships**.

You have another choice for organizing your business: the **Limited Liability Company** ("LLC"). You and your advisors may want to give the LLC very careful consideration, since it combines the income tax advantages of a partnership with the asset protection and limited liability of a regular "C" corporation. Furthermore, unlike an S corporation, the LLC is not restricted by limits on the type or number of stockholders.

Many S corporation owners and their advisors have undertaken a thorough review of S status, and concluded that the purported advantages are outweighed by the disadvantages. They have then converted their S corporations to C corporations. If you own an S corporation, ask your advisors to consider such a review.

Please see Chapter 7 for more information about Family Limited Partnerships and Limited Liability Companies.

* * *

If you decide to <u>sell</u> your business, the increased income generated by the Charitable Remainder Trust may provide the critical dollars that make the difference between a done deal, or no deal. You may be willing and able to lower the sale price, thanks to the larger stream of dollars generated by the Charitable Remainder Trust.

➢ Example: Fred and Ethel own Wonder Widget, Inc., a C corporation. At age 60, after 30 years of hard work, they want to sell the Corporation and pursue other interests. Working with Barney, a business broker, they determine that the Corporation is worth $2,500,000, including goodwill valued at $2,000,000. The goodwill and all of the other assets have a basis in Wonder Widget of $0. Fred and Ethel's basis in the Wonder Widget stock is $0.

➢ After consulting with their attorney and accountant, Fred and Ethel learn that an asset sale at $2,500,000 will leave them with approximately $1,320,000, after corporate and individual taxes. Invested to yield 7% net income, the sale proceeds would produce approximately $92,400 — before income tax. "Too low," says Fred. "Ask for $3,000,000," Ethel instructs Barney.

➤ Weeks go by, with no offers. "$3,000,000 is too high," says Barney.

➤ Finally comes an offer from Colossal Widget, Inc.— $2,500,000 worth of Colossal stock in exchange for the stock of Wonder. Fred and Ethel are about to reject the offer, when Barney gives them a copy of *Beyond Death & Taxes*, which he received at a seminar sponsored by an association of business brokers.

➤ Fred and Ethel read the book. Again they confer with Barney, their accountant, attorney, and now an insurance agent.

➤ Bottom line: a stock sale by a Charitable Remainder Trust, at $2,500,000, would result in no tax either upon the initial exchange of stock, or upon the subsequent sale of the Colossal stock. Investing the full $2,500,000 at 7%, the Charitable Remainder Trust can generate $175,000, before taxes.

➤ Result: the deal is done, for $2,500,000.

As you can see, using a Charitable Remainder Trust to structure the purchase and sale of a business will often be a win/win situation for both the Seller and the Buyer. Viewed in this perspective, *you should feel free to suggest the Charitable Remainder Trust strategy not only if you are the Seller, but also if you are the Buyer.* The same goes for the advisors of the Buyer and the Seller.

When it comes to buying or selling stock in a closely-held business, or land, or any other asset that does not have a readily ascertainable value, the Charitable Remainder Trust is an equal opportunity opportunity.

What if Fred and Ethel would like to have liquid assets outside the Charitable Remainder Trust? No problem— they could sell 10%, or 20%, or 50% of the stock to Colossal, outside the Charitable Remainder Trust. It would make no difference to Colossal.

Of course, Fred and Ethel would have a capital gains tax to pay with respect to any stock sold outside the Charitable Remainder Trust, offset in part by an income tax charitable deduction— if they were willing to preclude the possibility of the Remainder ever going to a Family Foundation. If they wanted the Remainder to go to a Family Foundation, their deduction for income tax purposes would be limited to their basis: zero. A Community Foundation could be the resolution. (Please see Chapter 6.)

Once again, they can choose between degrees of control and other benefits. So can you.

* * *

Why have we spent so much time plumbing the depths of selling your business through a Charitable Remainder Trust? Simply because you are entitled to know, before you give away one-fifth of the blood, sweat and tears that you put into that business, that *you have a choice*.

If you are a Buyer, you owe it to yourself.

Perhaps the more appropriate question would be: why would you ever sell your business— or any other valuable, appreciated asset— without first learning what a Charitable Remainder Trust can do for you, your family, and your community?

* * *

Land, stock in a closely-held business, and art work are all examples of **hard-to-value assets**, because each asset is unique and there is no ready market, such as a stock exchange, to set the value of the assets. Gifts to a Charitable Remainder Trust of this type of asset may require appraisal by an **independent qualified appraiser**. Such hard-to-value assets will also require the appointment of a Trustee other than the original creators of the Charitable Remainder Trust (the "Donors"). The **Independent Special Trustee** will have responsibility for administering the hard-to-value assets (until they are sold or otherwise transferred from the Trust). The Independent Special Trustee should not be an employee, paid advisor or immediate family member of the Donors.

Creation of a Charitable Remainder Trust is certainly not limited to large gifts of highly-appreciated property by

Donors who are in their sixties or seventies. For example, please see Chapter 8 for a description of how a Charitable Remainder Trust may be used as an alternative to **qualified retirement plans.**

Your Charitable Remainder Trust can be designed to optimize the timing of distributions of taxable income. Remember one of the golden rules of tax planning: if you have to pay a tax, defer the payment until you actually need the income. For example, with the right type of Charitable Remainder Trust, in your retirement years, you could receive income from a much larger base of Trust investments. In addition, you could receive all or a portion of the income to which you would have been entitled during the pre-retirement years when your Charitable Remainder Trust was invested for growth rather than income. This type of Trust is referred to as a **net income with make-up charitable remainder unitrust**, known in planning parlance as a **NIMCRUT**.

To illustrate, let us assume that when you are 65, the assets in your NIMCRUT have appreciated $200,000 in value, and that $200,000 could have been distributed to you in earlier years if it had been available in the form of net income. As Trustee, you now direct your Charitable Remainder Trust to invest in assets that generate income at a rate of 8%. If the pay-out rate for your Charitable Remainder Trust was 5%, you would be entitled to receive both the 5%, and the additional 3%, reducing your $200,000 " IOU account" by that 3%.

If the property to be transferred is **illiquid**, such as land, a painting, or stock in a closely-held business, a NIMCRUT has the advantage of avoiding any need for distributions, in case of a delay in the sale of the property. You should also consider a "flip" trust for this type of peroperty (more below).

* * *

As we have seen, the NIMCRUT offers great flexibility — with corresponding risk that the income and/or the value of the principal could decline, to the point that distributions could be severely diminished, if not eliminated altogether.

At the other end of the spectrum of predictable distribution is the **Charitable Remainder Annuity Trust**, often referred to as a **CRAT**. While the Roberts were considering what kind of Charitable Remainder Trust to create, they happened to be talking with a friend whose mother, Helen Troy, had just created a CRAT. Here's how:

➤ At age 75, Helen transferred publicly-traded stock worth $1,000,000 to her CRAT, with a 9% pay-out rate. The stock was paying a dividend of $20,000 per year.

➤ Every year for the rest of her life Helen would be entitled to receive $90,000 from her CRAT — regardless of whether the Trust investments increased or decreased in value, and regardless of net income. If net income were less than $90,000, the difference would be paid from principal.

If Helen wanted to contribute more property to a Charitable Remainder Trust, she would need to create another Charitable Remainder Trust, because a CRAT may receive only one gift.

As the Roberts' planning extended to other members of the family, Amelia's mother, Camille, also decided to create a CRAT. Camille's Trust named the Roberts Family Foundation as the remainderman— but we are getting ahead of the story.

Why would you NOT want to use a CRAT?

For one thing, although a CRAT has little or no downside in terms of the certainty of your receiving a fixed distribution, it has no upside, either. The amount of distribution will never increase, no matter how long you live or how much the buying power of a dollar may be eroded by inflation.

For many of his clients who were interested in a Charitable Remainder Trust, Frank Jones found that the **Standard Charitable Remainder Unitrust** (referred to as a "**SCRUT**") struck the best balance between predictability and flexibility. He and his team of advisors had constructed a SCRUT for the Jablonskis, Ronald and Marta.

From her parents, Marta had inherited a parcel of land that had been valued at $50,000 for estate tax purposes in her parents' estates. For 20 years the value of the property had meandered to a value of approximately $100,000. Then, literally overnight, the value had been catapulted by the announcement that a foreign car manufacturer was going to build a major industrial complex in the area where the property was located. Ronald and Marta had been approached by a developer who had made them an unsolicited offer of $1,000,000. At that point, <u>before any documents had been signed</u>, and before any other terms of the deal had been discussed or negotiated, Marta saw an article in her newspaper that described the benefits of using a Charitable Remainder Trust. When Marta asked her accountant, Susan Anderson, whether a Charitable Remainder Trust might be appropriate for them, Susan called Frank Jones and scheduled an appointment.

After careful analysis by the team of Susan, Frank, Dave Ryan, the insurance agent, and the Jablonskis' financial advisor, Fred Herman, the SCRUT emerged as the type of Charitable Remainder Trust best suited to the Jablonskis' goals and priorities.

Under the terms of the Jablonski SCRUT:

➤ A pay-out rate of 6% was selected.

➤ Fred told the Jablonskis that during the Jablonskis' life expectancies, investment in a diversified portfolio of balanced-growth mutual funds, could reasonably be expected to produce an <u>average</u> **total return** of between 8% and 10%, net of investment fees and other expenses.

➤ Since the pay-out rate of the Jablonskis' SCRUT would

only be 6%, if Fred's estimates proved accurate, the value of the Trust would grow at a rate likely to match or even exceed the rate of inflation.

➤ Compared to a CRAT, the proposed SCRUT offered Ronald and Marta a potential increase in annual distributions, while providing substantial protection against inflation. Since both Ronald and Marta had family histories of good health and longevity, the long-term flexibility of the SCRUT was important to them.

➤ Ronald and Marta felt comfortable with the understanding that distributions from a SCRUT did not have to depend upon the Trust investments generating a high level of income in the form of dividends or interest ("ordinary income"). For example, if their SCRUT generated ordinary income of 4%, the balance of the pay-out rate of 6% would be made up from the principal of the Trust, presumably from growth in the value of securities held in the Trust portfolio. Even though the SCRUT might have to sell securities in order to raise cash for the distribution, the SCRUT would pay no capital gains tax.

➤ Fred Herman liked the investment flexibility afforded by the Jablonskis' SCRUT, because he was free to search out the best long-term investments, regardless of how much or how little ordinary income they might produce. After consulting with the Jablonskis, he settled on an investment strategy that blended growth and income stocks. As one result, **virtually all of the distributions to the Jablonskis were taxed to them at a 15% federal rate.** Compared to a NIMCRUT distributing the same amount, the SCRUT design increased after-tax cash flow by over 20%.

* * *

As noted above, a "flip" Charitable Remainder Trust may facilitate the sale of hard-to-value property. For example, you transfer vacant land to a NIMCRUT. However, your prospective Buyer walks away. No problem—since your NIMCRUT generates no income, no distribution is required. Three months later, your Buyer comes back. The Trust converts, or "flips" to a SCRUT. Now the Trust will have liquid assets enabling it to make the required distributions.

* * *

Which type of Charitable Remainder Trust is right for you? There is no simple answer to this question. In fact, in most estate and business planning, you should be skeptical of "simple" answers. Even in situations where the current value of assets is relatively low, at the core of all effective estate and business planning must be a careful analysis of all of the relevant human and personal factors involved. After all, for each set of clients, life savings have the same relative value.

Charitable Remainder Trusts are an excellent illustration of the danger in seeking to use a single planning technique in a vacuum isolated from the full context of your circumstances. A Charitable Remainder Trust is not a product, or an end in itself, but rather one of several means of accomplishing your goals and priorities.

For some of you, <u>after</u> a thorough review of all planning issues and options, the SCRUT will emerge with a clear preference, as in the case of the Jablonskis. However, some clients having the identical fact pattern might be more comfortable with the NIMCRUT approach. Others for whom steady distributions are paramount would find most peace of mind with a CRAT.

In a number of situations, it will be feasible and appropriate for you to have <u>more than one</u> type of Charitable Remainder Trust, created simultaneously or over the course of many years.

If you foresee a significant possibility of using a Charitable Remainder Trust, consider establishing your Trust <u>as soon as possible</u>. The Trust can be initially funded with as little as $5,000, and maintained "on the shelf" for nominal annual fees. Then, whenever an opportunity arises to sell that appreciated property, the Trust is up and running, with no risk of your losing the sales opportunity. Instant access can be especially valuable if you are an executive who holds publicly-traded stock in your company. Such stock is generally subject to many restrictions on the timing and amount of sales.

Also bear in mind that if you give property to a Charitable Remainder Trust at a time when you are under a binding obligation to sell that property to a specific buyer, it is too late. If you transfer property to a Charitable Remainder Trust under those circumstances, and the property is then sold to that buyer, you will have to pay the capital gains tax—without the ability to use any of the proceeds from the sale! The time to transfer is when you are ready to sell and are reasonably confident that a willing and able buyer is at hand.

What if you learn about the benefits of a Charitable Remainder Trust just after you sign an enforceable Purchase and Sale Agreement? You believe that the Buyer would be willing to "tear up" the Agreement, and simply sign the identical Agreement with the Trust identified as the Seller. Is there any harm or risk in this approach? Yes, there is both harm and risk. First, to alter the facts in this manner would be unethical.

Second, Murphy's Law has not been repealed. Whether you are contemplating a Charitable Remainder Trust or any other tax planning technique, **the only prudent course is to assume that Uncle Sam is present for every discussion, and aware of every fact.** If someone supports a proposed arrangement with the argument that only a tiny fraction of tax returns are ever audited, remember Murphy, and move on to another plan.

Is there a down side to a Charitable Remainder Trust? YES. Once you transfer property to a Charitable Remainder Trust, with very limited exceptions you cannot ever receive the principal amount of that property. It bears repeating: **you should never ever transfer property to a Charitable Remainder Trust unless you are totally comfortable with the amount and liquidity of assets available to you outside of the Trust**.

You do have the flexibility of giving a <u>portion</u> of the appreciated asset to a Charitable Remainder Trust, thereby partially avoiding the capital gains tax when the Charitable Remainder Trust sells the asset. If you would like ready access to additional liquid assets, you can sell the rest of the appreciated asset <u>outside</u> of the Charitable Remainder Trust. This technique is sometimes referred to as a **split sale**. The sale of assets outside the Trust will trigger a capital gain, which may be offset partially or even entirely by your income tax deduction for the property you gave to the Charitable Remainder Trust. You <u>may</u> also be able to offset the gain by taking capital losses on other assets.

Remember that after you transfer a home, undeveloped land, or art works to a Charitable Remainder Trust, you may not use the property without severe tax consequences, due to the Internal Revenue Code rules against **self-dealing**. For example, you could not keep the art work at home.

* * *

Like the Roberts, you may find that the Charitable Remainder Trust offers a compelling blend of practical and charitable benefits.

For the Roberts, the compelling tax and economic advantages were only part of their motivation to create a Charitable Remainder Trust. The substantial gift that would be used for charitable purposes after their deaths was in perfect harmony with their living support of charitable organizations. The spiritual satisfaction they derived from knowing that $1,000,000 would eventually help build worthy causes was of great benefit to them.

For the Roberts' financial advisor, Fred Herman, the Charitable Remainder Trust was a boon. Once the Trust was funded, the investment goals set by the Roberts could be pursued with much less distortion from income tax considerations. With guidance from the Roberts, investments were selected, held and liquidated based primarily on economic merit.

So attractive were the investment advantages of Charitable Remainder Trusts that many of Fred's clients insisted upon using them, even though for some of them the charitable aspects were secondary.

Fred realized that other advantages could flow from the Charitable Remainder Trust. In addition to earning fees or commissions for his services to the Trust itself, he could look forward to the possibility of earning income from two other pools of wealth—

- The Roberts Family Foundation (potentially $7,000,000 or more), and

- The Roberts Wealth Replacement Trust (potentially $3,000,000 or more).

True, it might be many years before there were significant assets in these two pools, but Fred took the long view. He was interested in <u>building relationships</u>, not merely in the isolated transaction. If he continued to provide excellent service to the Roberts family, some day either he or his firm would be able to convert goodwill into additional services for the Foundation and the Trust. *Without the New Estate Planning, these opportunities would never have existed.*

Another powerful appeal of the Charitable Remainder Trust for the Roberts was that <u>they were in control</u>. They could be the Trustees. As Trustees they could hire and replace the investment advisors, and determine the investment program. They also liked the fact that, at any time, they could change the designation of the charitable organization(s) that would eventually receive the Remainder of the Trust.

* * *

Of course, as Frank Jones (the family attorney) was careful to point out, the Trustees of a Charitable Remainder Trust had to comply with their **fiduciary duties**, just like the Trustees of any other type of Trust. For example, if they were to invest in highly risky stocks, resulting in huge losses, the charitable remainderman (or the state attorney general) might seek to recover the losses from their estates. As Trustees, it was also vital that Charles and Amelia work closely with their team of advisors to be sure that all i's were dotted and t's crossed.

* * *

Despite the way advantages of a Charitable Remainder Trust, there was one concern that Amelia and Charles confided to their attorney, Frank Jones. Over a long span of time, how could they be certain that the charitable organizations that they ultimately designated would carry out their charitable goals? After all, they were well aware of dramatic shifts in the direction and reliability of even the most revered charitable organizations.

Sally and Neil also understood the theory and operation of the Charitable Remainder Trust. They readily agreed it made good sense from an economic perspective and that it helped to fulfill the charitable values they shared with their parents. Yet they had to admit that they were troubled by the prospect that $1,000,000 or more of family property might eventually be beyond their control. Neil called Frank to get his thoughts.

It was at this point in our story that the Roberts family met the Roberts Family Foundation.

CHARITABLE REMAINDER TRUST
(With Wealth Replacement Trust)

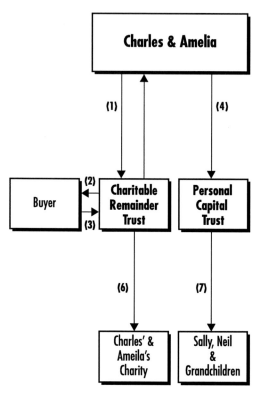

1 Charles and Amelia transfer asset to Charitable Trust and receive income tax deduction

2 Trustee sells asset for cash and pays no capital gains tax

3 Cash received by Trustee

4 Income flow and tax savings to Charles and Amelia enable them to make gifts to Personal Capital Trust, for funding insurance premiums

5 Income and estate tax free inheritance for Neil, Sally and grandchildren

6 Gift to Charles' and Amelia's charity (Family foundation)

GRAPHIC II

6 BUILDING WITH FOUNDATIONS

I n this chapter we will learn about a critical link in Total Wealth Control: organizations that allow several generations of a family to *connect and direct their Community Capital to their communities.*

* * *

A **Private Foundation** is a form of charitable organization. Assuming that a private foundation follows certain rules provided by the Internal Revenue Code, it will not be subject to federal or state income tax.

Your Private Foundation can:

➤ Be completely controlled by your family (a "Family Foundation").

➤ Engage in its own active, charitable program; it can select, organize and carry out its charitable activities.

➤ In addition, or in the alternative, it can channel income from its investments to other charitable organizations.

* * *

The charitable organizations that won the support of the Roberts and The Roberts Family Foundation came to realize that *deferred* giving did not have to decrease *current gifts*. To the contrary, the Charitable Remainder Trust provided these organizations with a golden opportunity to reinforce the family's awareness of their mission and programs. Instead of seeking only large, irrevocable gifts from donors, these enlightened organizations prized the opportunity to build voluntary on-going relationships with the donors. Once again, less "control" over donors meant *more support in the long run.*

* * *

"Neil? Are you there?"

Frank Ryan's increased volume on the telephone startled Neil Roberts. Having been satisfied by Frank's answers to his questions about control of the Roberts Family Foundation, Neil had found himself musing about certain charitable activities that he might propose for the Foundation. As a real estate developer, he had come to have a keen interest in the subtle and complex relationships between ownership of homes, human values and property values. For several years, Neil had been active with a charitable organization that provided money and professional expertise which enabled community groups to acquire and manage their own housing. The results were in stunning contrast to those of an earlier era, in which large housing projects were constructed and managed by government agencies. When residents owned their own homes, however humble, pride replaced graffiti and broken glass.

The confidence that came from the complex process of reclaiming and rehabilitating dilapidated housing generated ripples of confidence in many other directions, both from and towards the recovering community. Business and academic institutions were attracted to communities that demonstrated an ability to salvage their own housing. Perhaps the Roberts Family Foundation could become a force in building more housing partnerships among community residents, businesses, government and academia.

"Yes, Frank, I am still here."

* * *

Following their various consultations, Neil Roberts and Sally Roberts were confident that the Roberts Family Foundation would be a source of enormous benefit to their community, and to several generations of the Roberts family. For Amelia Roberts, the Family Foundation represented a logical and deeply satisfying culmination of the planning that had been done by the family and their advisors.

Amelia contemplated the Roberts Family Foundation with many emotions. She was grateful that her family supported her commitment to charitable activities. She was excited at the prospect of the family working more closely together and with organizations in the community to identify new ways of helping people to help themselves.

Yet Amelia was concerned, on behalf of Charles. One memorable Thanksgiving, Amelia and the children had told Charles of their strong support for the Family Foundation. Charles had been silent during most of the conversation, as he listened to the reasons, doubts, and resolutions exchanged by the other family members. When Neil and Sally left, in the quiet of the study, Charles stood up and began methodically pacing back and forth between the window and the fireplace. Now, as night was falling, it was Amelia's turn to listen. Charles began one of his signature soliloquies, in which he meticulously assembled and examined all sides of an issue, carefully avoiding a conclusion until every facet had been considered. Flickers from the fire punctuated his words.

"Frank and I had a good talk about these matters earlier this week," Charles was saying. Amelia nodded and rocked and knitted a sweater for one of her granddaughters. "Frank and I went over the concepts and the nuts and bolts of using the Family Foundation as the centerpiece of our Total Wealth Control. I think that all of us in the family agree that it is the right thing for us to do." Amelia nodded and knitted.

"Frank also asked me the hard question, the one that I

have been approaching and avoiding for several years. What would I like to do with the rest of my days? I am tempted to continue just what I have been doing— running the business until I stop running. There are some very exciting opportunities for our Company, down the information highway. Leading the Company in pursuit of those opportunities would be satisfying, I am sure, but I hear the clock ticking," at which point the grandfather clock chimed. "I would like to take whatever skills and wisdom I may have acquired, and work with you, Sally and Neil, and others, to give people some of the same opportunities that I have enjoyed. I think that the Foundation is exactly what I have been looking for."

Stopping by the bookshelves, Charles pulled out a well-worn volume of Carl Sandburg's monumental biography of Abraham Lincoln. "I do not think that I have any delusions of immortality, but I do believe that with all of our family resources our Foundation can help to make a difference. You know this biography of Lincoln?" Amelia looked up and nodded. She purled.

"In these volumes Sandburg sings a hymn to the vision, the courage and the drive of the ordinary American— the triumph of the American spirit. Given half an opportunity, and left to their own ingenuity, Americans keep coming closer to the ideal of the community helping each individual to realize his full potential." "Or her potential," gently added Amelia.

Charles glanced over at Amelia, and nodded, "Yes, her potential, too. In our own small way, our family can be an active part of that tradition." Charles resumed his methodical pacing, now in a triangular pattern. "I am not going to retreat or retire. I am going to charge. The Foundation will help this family keep growing together, and help our community to come closer together."

Coming to a stop by the window, Charles' silhouette flickered in the light from the fire. "How's that for a revelation?" he asked with a chuckle. Amelia nodded. Carefully she put down her knitting and turned out the light.

* * *

When both Charles and Amelia are gone, Sally and Neil will run the Roberts Family Foundation. As Trustees, they will be entitled to receive reasonable compensation for their services to the Foundation. <u>Depending upon the nature and extent of their services</u>, the annual compensation could be one to three percent of the value of the Foundation assets.

In addition to any funds contributed by the Roberts during their lifetimes, upon the death of the survivor of Charles and Amelia the Foundation would be funded from two sources:

> ➤ The Foundation would receive all of the property remaining in the Roberts Charitable Remainder Trust.

> ➤ The Foundation would receive the remaining estates

of Charles and Amelia, reduced by any of their remaining Estate Tax Exclusions.

You can see the Roberts Family Foundation in Graphic III, at the end of this Chapter.

As Frank Jones, the Roberts' attorney, contemplated the intricate yet flexible web of connections between the Roberts family and their business, he marveled again at the conventional wisdom that all too often erects a Great Wall between "business law" and "estate planning," as though these were two alien worlds, until it is too late. So many lost opportunities, so many devastating— and avoidable— consequences. The conventional approach reminded Frank of the riddle: what is the sound of one hand clapping?

The Roberts and their advisors estimated that the Foundation would eventually contain approximately $7,000,000. Since Family Foundations are generally required to distribute at least 5% of their value annually, the family anticipated that each year they would have $350,000 for the support of charitable activities and organizations in their community.

What charitable organizations or activities would you support with $350,000 a year? *What impact would those dollars have in your community?* How would your community reach out to you and your Foundation?

Remember: under their original plan the Roberts would have sent over $4,000,000 *anonymous* and *invisible* dollars to the government in estate taxes.

* * *

A Family Foundation can be your vehicle for *visible, voluntary philanthropy*, with the potential for profound *impact* upon a carefully selected group of charities and the people whom they serve.

The Roberts chose the most active form of voluntary philanthropy: direct charitable activities staffed and managed by the Family Foundation itself. The Foundation would hire attorneys, accountants and other advisors as needed. You may choose to do as the Roberts have done. *You also have other choices.*

For example, you and your family can choose a **donor-advised fund**. The donor-advised fund has these characteristics:

> ➤ The fund is managed by a charitable organization called a **Community Foundation**.

> ➤ A Community Foundation usually has deep involvement in a particular community, though it may also serve other communities. Some Community Foundations operate nationally.

> ➤ The Community Foundation has professional employees who are responsible for the administration of funds gathered from many donors.

> ➤ The Community Foundation meets regularly and confers with the adult children of the original donors regarding their choices for the distribution of the income from the family fund.

Although the Community Foundation technically has the final say concerning distributions, the tradition of such arrangements reveals great sensitivity to the wishes of the donor family.

The growth of Community Foundations is explosive. The growth is fueled in part because Community Foundations provide donors with the benefit of control, combined with freedom from administrative burdens. The Community Foundation may be especially appealing when the charitable fund is <u>relatively</u> small, in the $1,000,000 to $5,000,000 range. Under current law, the Community Foundation may also allow you to obtain a significantly higher income tax charitable deduction than if you opt for a Family Foundation. Furthermore, since the Community Foundation is a **public charity**, it does not have to pay the 1% or 2% annual **excise tax** required of Family Foundations.

Another force is driving the popularity of Community Foundations: the renaissance of grass roots optimism and commitment. We are returning to the tradition of local solutions for local problems. Community Foundations keep dollars working in your own Community. They also facilitate personal connection and participation, along with accountability. We can see the results of our good intentions. We can move more quickly to improve programs, or to shift resources to the programs that are doing the best job. We can measure the tangible return on our investment of

Community Capital.

Does <u>your</u> community have a Community Foundation? If not, perhaps you could help to start one.

* * *

Another form of family-directed charity is the **support organization**. Say that your family were interested in supporting a particular nonprofit hospital. You and the Hospital form a support organization with a board of Directors having nine members. Four members are apointed by your family, and five are appointed by the Hospital. In a strict legal sense, the Hospital does have majority control, but it is likely to be very responsive to the goals and concerns of your family. In return, since the support organization is treated as a public charity, your family's lifetime contributions may qualify for a larger charitable income tax deduction, and/or more rapid use of the deduction. Also, the excise tax imposed on the income of private foundations will not apply.

A support organization may also align itself with a Community Foundation, which would enable the family to support a broad spectrum of charitable activities and organizations.

* * *

Once again, depending upon your priorities, in managing your family's Community Capital you will choose between various degrees of control, and other benefits.

In the realm of Community Capital, the rising tide of the Community Foundation may come to be the equivalent of the corporation in the realm of traditional investments: a vehicle that permits many individuals with relatively small amounts of capital to join forces in the enterprise of solving community problems. Of course, there is one significant difference: when you and your family "invest" in a Community Foundation, the family may exercise a high degree of control over its investments, no matter how large the Foundation may be.

In lieu of an ongoing Family Charity, it may be perfectly satisfactory to direct your Community Capital outright to one or more charitable organizations, no strings attached. The estate tax savings and the renewable stream of community benefits will be the same.

For Charles and Amelia, however, and for their children, the Roberts Family Foundation offered a unique, personal, and enduring expression of their wish to return good fortune to their community. **The Family Foundation fuses "family" with "charity."**

Every year at Thanksgiving, the Roberts clan would gather at the home of Charles and Amelia. Once the Foundation had been established, the Thanksgiving tradition included an evening meeting in their living room, lit at first by a single candle. Each member of the family, including some very young Roberts, would then take a turn proposing an activity for the Foundation to support. As each proposal was made, another candle was lit from the original candle.

* * *

How long will you have the philanthropic opportunities that were available to the Roberts? In their present form the Charitable Remainder Trust and the Family Foundation were approved by Congress in 1969. The laws governing these Trusts and Foundations have changed very little since that time. These arrangements have become an integral part of the fabric of charitable giving in the United States.

As for private foundations, there are now more than sixty thousand in existence, with assets exceeding four hundred seventy seven billion dollars.

True, Congress could take away what it has given. However, a drastic reversal in the charitable system seems unlikely as long as self-help and local initiative are at a premium. With a decline in government support and intervention, *the need for charitable organizations has never been stronger.*

Studies have shown that for every tax dollar "lost" to charitable deductions, *that dollar is more than replaced by the value of services generated by charitable organizations.*

Remember also that the government will have an opportunity to tax any income distributed to you from the Charitable Remainder Trust— income that might not have been generated and become taxable without the use of the Trust.

Finally, if the laws were changed, such changes would not reverse tax benefits already received. Existing Charitable Remainder Trusts and Family Foundations would likely be largely if not entirely exempted from the changes. When you use a Charitable Remainder Trust, you achieve the great economic advantage— elimination of the capital gains tax— just as soon as the appreciated property is sold by your Trust.

Effective May 5, 2003, the federal capital gains tax rate for most (but not all) assets was lowered from 20% to 15%.

However, viewed in the context of Total Wealth Control, the Charitable Remainder Trust still offers unique advantages, compared to the outright sale of an asset:

➤ Substantial tax savings that keep working for you, for the rest of your life. On the sale of a $1,000,000 asset with a zero basis, you will save $150,000 in federal tax. Assuming a payout rate of 8%, that would mean an additional $12,000 every year, until the death of you and your spouse. State tax savings may generate additional cash flow.

➤ The possibility of substantial income tax savings, thanks to the charitable income tax deduction.

➤ The ability to invest the entire proceeds from the sale

in a tax-free environment.

➤ Asset protection, at least for the principal in the Trust.

➤ With a NIMCRUT, the ability to defer taxable income until you need it.

➤ The enhanced opportunity to provide current or future support to one or more charitable organizations during your lifetime, and the recognition that flows from such support.

Fluctuations in the capital gains tax rate are ultimately nothing more or less than one of a myriad of variables for you and your advisors to consider— and then to apply to your best advantage.

THE ROBERTS FAMILY FOUNDATION

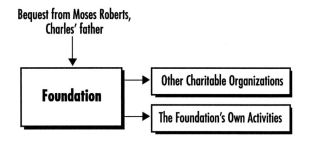

Bequest from Moses Roberts,
Charles' father

Foundation

Other Charitable Organizations

The Foundation's Own Activities

During Charles' and Amelia's Lifetimes
- ► Charles and Amelia have control
- ► Neil, Sally and the grandchildren take an active role
- ► The family builds connections with the Community
- ► Foundation must distribute 5% of its value annually

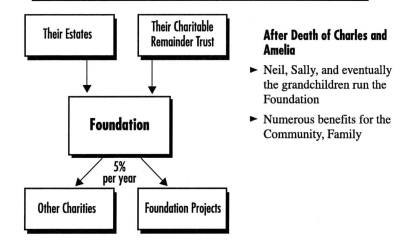

Their Estates

Their Charitable Remainder Trust

After Death of Charles and Amelia
- ► Neil, Sally, and eventually the grandchildren run the Foundation
- ► Numerous benefits for the Community, Family

Foundation

5%
per year

Other Charities

Foundation Projects

GRAPHIC III

7 THE FAMILY LIMITED PARTNERSHIP OR LIMITED LIABILITY COMPANY

A s the years went by, the Roberts saw dark clouds gathering over their beloved second home, Blue Mountain.

Charles and Amelia had already used a **conservation easement** to protect a large portion of Blue Mountain. Still, the restricted portion of Blue Mountain continued to increase in value, to the point where it could easily be worth more than $1,000,000 by the time both Charles and Amelia had died. In addition, the 20-acre lot where the Roberts' second home was located would also continue to appreciate.

Although it seemed likely that the Wealth Replacement Trust could afford to buy Blue Mountain from the estates of Charles and Amelia, the increasing values would create financial pressure on their children and other heirs, who would be faced with ongoing costs of maintaining and repairing the structures on the property, paying property taxes and so forth. The problem posed by these costs is sometimes referred to as **the "endowment" problem**.

Meanwhile, there was another asset that the Roberts

wished to preserve: Roberts Electronics. The Company was already worth several million dollars, with good prospects for further appreciation, but further appreciation also meant additional estate tax pressure at a tax rate of 50% or more. Once again, with conventional planning Uncle Sam was a silent but very powerful partner.

Discussing these concerns at one of their regular meetings with Neil, Sally and their advisors, the Roberts recalled one of the **basic strategies** of their planning. Once the Roberts had established the Wealth Replacement Trust, funded with life insurance, to assure the desired level of Personal Capital for their children and grandchildren, Charles and Amelia intended to **transfer additional property to the younger generations during their lifetimes, with a minimum of transfer tax.**

That meeting was the origin of the Roberts Family Limited Partnership-I. Here is how it worked:

➤ Frank Jones, the family attorney, drew up a Limited Partnership Agreement. The General Partner was Blue Mountain, Inc., a "C" corporation. All of the stock in this corporation was issued to Charles and Amelia, in exchange for their **capital contribution.** The General Partner managed the Limited Partnership. Blue Mountain, Inc. owned a 1% **General Partner Interest** in the Partnership, purchased with cash.

➤ The Roberts then transferred 20 buildable lots of Blue Mountain land to the Partnership. Before discounting (see below), the lots were valued at $600,000.

➤ In exchange for the lots, the Roberts received all of

the **Limited Partner Interests** in the Roberts Family Limited Partnership-I representing 99% of the total interest in the Partnership.

➤ No gift tax was due on the transfer of the land to the Partnership.

➤ The Roberts created an Irrevocable Generation-Skipping Trust, as to which they were the Donors. They transferred all of their Limited Partner Interests to the Trust, by gift. The beneficiaries of the Trust were their children, grandchildren, and any future issue.

You can see the Roberts Family Limited Partnership-I in Graphic IV at the end of this Chapter.

For gift tax purposes, the Roberts were able to **discount** or lower the value of the Limited Partner Interests by 25%, because there was no ready way to sell these Interests, and the Interests had limited voting rights. Furthermore, the Limited Partners were "locked in"— they had no right to withdraw cash or other property from the Partnership, until the Partnership was terminated. Taken together, these factors are sometimes referred to collectively as the **minority discount**.

After discounting, the net value of the gift was $450,000. (The Courts have allowed larger discounts for Limited Partner Interests, but the Roberts and their advisors preferred a more conservative course.)

➤ The Roberts paid no gift tax on this transfer, since they were able to apply $450,000 of their combined Gift Tax Exclusions.

➤ During their lifetimes, Charles and Amelia had complete control of the Partnership, by virtue of their owning all of the stock in the General Partner.

➤ On their gift tax return, the Roberts allocated $450,000 of their combined $3,000,000 GST Exemptions to the gift. From that point forward, the Trust property could be sheltered from several generations of potential estate tax-- regardless of the amount of future increase in the value of the Blue Mountain lots.

In addition to the gift of Limited Partner Interests, since the Roberts had applied $800,000 of their GST Exemptions to their gifts to the Personal Capital Trust (see Chapter 4), they would still have $1,750,000 of unused GST Exemptions available for transfers of other property.

The Roberts could have chosen to transfer some of the Limited Partner Interests by using Annual Gifts, thereby preserving some portion of their Gift Tax Exclusions for gifts of other property. As it happened, they made full use of their Annual Gifts by making gifts from their publicly-traded stock portfolio, together with their cash gifts, to the Personal Capital Trust, which also owned insurance on their lives.

Upon their deaths, the Roberts provided in their Wills and Revocable Trusts that their stock in Blue Mountain, Inc., would be left in equal shares to their son, Neil, and their daughter, Sally. Neil and Sally would then have equal control over the General Partner.

* * *

As for transferring shares of Roberts Electronics, Inc., to a Family Limited Partnership, Frank was very dubious. A Family Limited Partnership whose sole activity consisted of holding stock in a family business would not be considered <u>itself</u> to be engaged in a trade or business. Under IRS audit, that type of partnership could turn into a porcupine.

Were there alternatives for protecting Robert Elections?

"Weren't you thinking of starting some new product lines?" asked Frank.

"Yes," said Charles. "We were also thinking of expanding our retail operations, at some new locations."

Frank saw a glimmer. *"What if you were to organize these new operations in the form of one or more Family Limited Partnerships?* Most of the interests in these new Partnerships could be held by Irrevocable Generation-Skipping Trusts having the same design as the Trust that we created for the Roberts Family Limited Partnership-I. Blue Mountain, Inc., or perhaps another C corporation, could serve as the General Partner, which would give the two of you a high degree of control over the operations. For gift tax purposes, there would be little or no value in these new businesses. However, if the new Partnerships prosper, none of the increase in value would be subject to transfer tax, for several generations. Furthermore, if some day you had an

---

opportunity to sell the business, or to make a public offering of stock in the business, all of the family's business entities could be rebundled. Would you be interested?"

Charles and Amelia glanced at each other, then nodded in agreement.

In due course, a series of new businesses were created using the Family Limited Partnership technique. In addition, Charles and Amelia used their Annual Gifts to transfer stock in Roberts Electronics to Irrevocable Generation-Skipping Trusts for the benefit of their children and younger heirs.

* * *

If the advantages of a Family Limited Partnership sound appealing, ask your advisors to take you on a dry run of this familiar technique.

While you are at it, ask your advisors to compare the Family Limited Partnership with the **Limited Liability Company ("LLC")**. The LLC is something new under the sun, now available in all states.

Instead of "partners," an LLC has "Members." The LLC offers the tax advantages of a partnership, as well as limited liability for the investors who are not actively involved in the business. However, if you are the General Partner of a Family Limited Partnership, you will be exposed to **personal liaibility** for the debts or other liabilities of the Partnership. You may avoid or at least reduce the risk of that liability if you form a corporation to act as the General Partner. However, if you have an LLC, you will be protected by limited liability even if you are the **Managing Member**. You can avoid the expense and complication of creating and maintaining a corporate General Partner.

Whether you choose a Family Limited Partnership or an LLC as the vehicle for your family business, you have another transfer technique at your disposal. Suppose that you have made full use of your Annual Gifts and your Gift Tax Exclusion, yet you still own interests in the family business that are likely to increase in value. If you make an additional gift of these interests, you will owe gift tax. Instead, you may sell the Interests to the Irrevocable Trust that already owns Interests by reason of your previous gifts. The sale price reflects the same discount that you used to value the Interests for gift tax purposes. In return, you receive a Promisory Note, which will provide you with cash flow over several years.

So far, so good. You have shifted future growth out of your taxable estate, you have kept control of the business, and you have created cash flow. But wait–what about capital ain tax? If the Irrevocable Trust is a "grantor trust", you will not have any capital gain, and therefore no tax. You may engineer a grantor trust in many ways, e.g., by including your spouse as a beneficiary.

***

The Family Limited Partnership proved to be a powerful tool for the Roberts. It provided a very efficient way to carry out the **second basic planning strategy: transferring property during their lifetimes, at a discount, and with significant asset protection.**

FAMILY LIMITED PARTNERSHIP

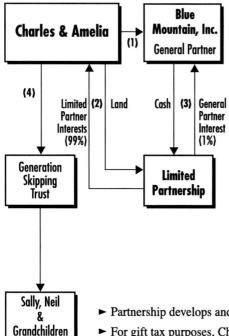

1 Charles and Amelia create and own Blue Mountain, Inc., a C corporation

2 Other assets are transferred to a Limited Partnership in return for Limited Partner Interests

3 Blue Mountain, Inc. purchases the General Partner Interest

4 Charles and Amelia gift the Limited Partner Interests to Generation Skipping Trust

► Partnership develops and sells land

► For gift tax purposes, Charles and Amelia will be entitled to discount 25% or more

► Can be used for Annual Exclusions and/or Gift Tax Credit Gifts

► Charles and Amelia retain control, by owning General Partner

► C corporation as General Partner limits liability

► Creditor protection for Trust assets

GRAPHIC IV

8 THE MIRAGE OF RETIREMENT PLANS

harles Roberts was known and admired for his steady temperment. Even during critical moments in business negotiations, he was rarely flustered, no matter how provocative the other parties might be. When words and reason failed, Charles limited himself to a severe glare. This morning, however, as he sat in a conference room in his accountant's office, Charles was seriously perturbed.

Susan Anderson had just led Charles through a concise and devastating analysis of the way in which his substantial retirement plan benefits were going to be confiscated by a series of taxes.

Susan looked at her client with concern and sympathy. Who could blame Charles for righteous indignation? For years Congress had encouraged business owners like Charles, as well as all other persons with substantial earned income, to contribute heavily every year to their **qualified retirement plans**. In the beginning, all was paradise: contributions to the plan were <u>deductible</u>, subject to reasonable limits. Distributions were taxed at capital gains rates. Also attractive was the fact that any plan assets remaining in the participant's account at the time of death were <u>not subject to estate tax</u>.

Under these enticing rules, the money poured in, trillions of dollars. Somewhere along the line, the tide reversed. Congress began to restrict or eliminate tax advantages. In the meantime, the Employee Retirement Income Security Act of 1974 ("ERISA"), a set of measures designed to protect the rights of pension plan participants, mushroomed in complexity. Congress spawned new statutory trolls with nicknames like TEFRA, DEFRA and REA. Ironically, these good intentions have succeeded in causing many employers to terminate their qualified retirement plans.

Susan glanced at the final slide she had just presented to Charles. For quite some time she had been warning Charles that the vaunted sanctuary of retirement plan benefits was under siege.

Susan's presentation went something like this—

NOTE: the "slides" you are about to see have been modified to simulate an actual slide presentation, and to minimize technical detail. Your advisors will be happy— or at least prepared— to fill in those details.

Susan's Slide Show
Qualified Retirement Plans: Miracle or Mirage?

➢ As vehicles for <u>accumulating</u> funds, your qualified retirement plans have been **POWERFUL ENGINES**—

➢ Your qualified contributions are not taxed;

➤ Inside the plans, generated income is exempt from income tax

BUT

Beware the gauntlet of taxes that await <u>distribution</u> of funds!

➤ *Income tax* on all distributions to plan participants (at current rates)

➤ 10% *penalty* for withdrawal prior to age 59 1/2

➤ When you pass away, no "step-up" in basis

➤ <u>Distributions to surviving beneficiaries are subject to income tax</u>

➤ If you name your surviving spouse as beneficiary, no estate tax due until his/her death

➤ When your surviving spouse passes away, any remaining benefits are subject to *estate tax*

➤ Benefits distributed to your children are subject to income tax, then estate tax in <u>their</u> estates

➤ Benefits passing to your grandchildren may be subject to *generation-skipping tax*

➤ **Worst case: $1 means only 15¢ for your grandchildren!**

When Charles had taken a sip of water and given the "15¢" slide a glare that could melt glass, Susan continued her slide presentation:

SALVAGING YOUR RETIREMENT PLAN

➤ Charles may make annual withdrawals to use as gifts to a Personal Capital Trust that owns joint life insurance

➤ Income tax will be due, but all other taxes <u>may</u> be eliminated!

➤ Designate Amelia as beneficiary for any remaining benefits

➤ Deferral of estate tax upon Charles' death

➤ Rollover to IRA will perpetuate income tax exemption

➤ After age 70 1/2, Amelia will begin taking required minimum distribution

➤ Amelia designates the Roberts Family Foundation as beneficiary upon her death

➤ *Eliminates estate tax*

➤ *Eliminates income tax*

➤ Distributions to charity not subject to income tax

➤ Fully compatible with your Total Wealth Control

➤ Consider a Charitable Remainder Trust (CRT) as an alternative accumulation vehicle

➤ Also consider CRT as **primary beneficiary** of plan benefits

➤ CRT for Amelia qualifies for estate tax deductions

➤ As the beneficiary of the CRT, Amelia has much more

control and flexibility regarding distributions

➤ No minimum distribution required

➤ Upon Amelia's passing away, leave remaining CRT property to Roberts Family Foundation

➤No estate tax

Susan enlivened the slide show with numerous charts and other graphics.

* * *

Susan turned on the lights.

For a long while Charles sat sunken in thought. He kept seeing the image of beautiful green apples in his orchard, turning brown as they fell to the earth. He enjoyed a fair fight, but this did not strike him as fair. The asault on retirement plans also struck him as very poor policy, since the rise of the baby boomers and other demographic indicators would seem to demand that the government <u>bolster</u> rather than <u>attack</u> incentives for private financing of retirement.

How many Americans were confident that Social Security and the Tooth Fairy would be there when it was their turn to retire? Who in Congress would be happy to explain to these Americans that the cupboard was bare?

Was it any wonder that employers were terminating their retirement plans right and left?

"Spilled milk," thought Charles. He was back in control.

He spent a good half hour reviewing the wreckage with Susan, and then a full hour dissecting the alternatives. Gradually he saw that Total Wealth Control pointed the way to a resolution that was entirely consistent with the existing spirit and structure of the Roberts' earlier planning.

There were the usual rounds of further consultations, involving Amelia, Neil, Sally, and the other Advisors.

Here is how the Roberts re-engineered the arrangement formerly and euphemistically known as their "qualified retirement plan:"

➤ At age 59 1/2, Charles began withdrawing annual distributions from his plan in an amount that enabled Amelia and Charles to pay income tax on the distributions and then to make additional gifts to their Personal Capital Trust. The Trust acquired additional joint life insurance on Charles and Amelia, to assure the Minimum Personal Capital for their heirs.

➤ A Charitable Remainder Trust (CRT) was the primary beneficiary of the retirement plan benefits. The CRT provided Amelia with cash flow for the rest of her life.

➤ Amelia designated the Roberts Family Foundation as the Primary Beneficiary of the CRT. The distribution of the CRT in one lump sum to the Foundation would be sheltered from estate tax by the unlimited estate tax charitable deduction.

➤ Since the Foundation was exempt for income tax purposes, it would pay no income tax upon receiving the distribution from the CRT.

The Roberts converted their retirement plans from a tax

disaster into a powerful engine for Total Wealth Control.

You have the same choice.

Please see Graphic V for the Roberts' retirement plan.

THE ROBERTS NEW RETIREMENT PLAN

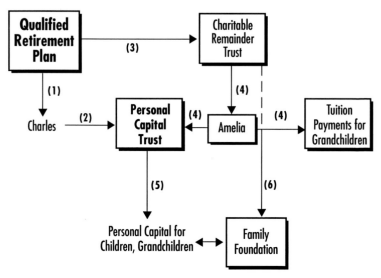

1 Charles receives distributions from Plan, pays income tax

2 Charles makes gifts to Personal Capital Trust

3 Upon Charles' death, Plan benefits are transferred to CRT

4 Amelia receives desired level of income from CRT, pays income tax, uses funds for gifts to Personal Capital Trust and/or tuitions.

5 Upon Amelia's death, insurance proceeds fill Personal Capital Trust.

6 Upon Amelia's death, Charitable Remainder Trust distributes all assets to Roberts Family Foundation

GRAPHIC V

9 CLOSING THE CIRCLE

Charles did not need to hear the words. On that freezing February morning, the look in Dr. O'Reilly's eyes told him that his worst fears were confirmed. The tumor was malignant, and spreading rapidly.

Charles felt a terrible lack of control. He had little time left, and so much that he wanted to do. For several weeks he experienced a deep depression, despite the love and comfort of his family.

The depression lifted one day when his grandson, Eli, bounded into Charles' darkened bedroom. At age five, Eli understood that his grandfather was very sick. He tried, with some success, to be very quiet around Charles. However, the lively sense of awe and wonder that Eli had inherited from Charles and Amelia was irresistible. "Granddaddy, come here! Come with me!" he exclaimed.

Charles heard his grandson's call coming from a great distance. When Eli tugged at his hand, Charles stifled an urge to growl, and laboriously hauled himself out of bed. Eli led him to the window, where Eli parted the blinds with his small paw. "Snow!"

Through his medicinal haze, Charles looked and saw, as though for the first time, the miracle of the feathery flakes. He opened the blinds and together Eli and Charles silently watched the orchard filling with snow.

From that moment Charles took charge. He recalled the process of his father's last days, and set about to put his life in the best possible order. He held meetings with his advisors. Charles drafted detailed memoranda of suggestions regarding the business, the Foundation, and many other matters. He met with key employees. Legal documents were revised as necessary.

Heeding advice from Frank Jones, the family attorney, and Susan Anderson, the family accountant, Charles and Amelia had already exchanged assets so that Charles owned virtually all of the assets that had a low basis. Upon his death, these assets would all be included in his estate, thereby receiving a step-up in basis and enabling the estate to sell those assets without incurring capital gains tax on the appreciation that had occurred before Charles' death.

Charles listened to Bach and Mozart. He met with friends and wrote many letters. He kept a journal. He had many long discussions with John Winthrop, his minister. His vision of the Family Foundation, already up and running, gave him deep satisfaction. In addition to providing for Amelia and the rest of his family, Charles had helped to create a living legacy for his community.

With the end coming near, Charles spent most of his

time with different family members. Tears and favorite stories flowed freely.

* * *

Amelia peered out the kitchen window at her garden. She was delighted to see purple crocuses poking through the earth. She hurried to share the first rite of spring with Charles.

* * *

Charles lay still in the early morning light. Just outside his bedroom window, a chickadee was celebrating the warmth of the new season. Charles closed his eyes, held Amelia's steady hand, and took his leave.

* * *

Sunlight flooded into the Roberts living room on that morning in May, twenty years after Charles had passed away. Waiting for Amelia to join them, Neil, Sally and each of the family advisors felt a sense of accomplishment as they considered the progression of the planning process. There had been serious challenges and more than a few deep doubts along the way. Other families may well have made other choices, but the group gathered in that room could take comfort in knowing that they had explored, considered and acted on all of the available alternatives. *That is the essence of Total Wealth Control.*

For the Roberts family, the process had been as important as the results. They had derived great satisfaction from being active participants in designing their own evolving plan, rather than being the passive objects of the legal system.

Still, there was a large question hovering in the room that morning. Not about Amelia's health— that came one day at a time.

Now, the open question was: What had Amelia decided to do about Total Wealth Control? She planned to explain her intentions at the meeting, and to gather the opinions of her family and advisors before proceeding. Would she leave all of the property under her control to the Roberts Family Foundation? Perhaps she wished to include other charities with which she had been active recently. She might have a set of specific guidelines for the Foundation. Everyone was eager to hear her latest vision.

After Charles Roberts' death, the amount of property that would go to the Roberts Family Foundation was always subject to Amelia's control. By amending her Will and Revocable Trust, and by exercising the limited power of appointment she held over the Marital Trusts created by Charles, Amelia could direct any portion of the $7,000,000 remaining in her estate and in the Marital Trusts to the children (or other heirs) through the taxable route of conventional planning. She could also decide to leave 100% of the property to the Foundation, or 50%, or nothing at all. (Upon her death, the assets in the Charitable Remainder Trust would automatically pass to a charitable organization — presumably the Roberts Family Foundation. However, Amelia controlled the choice of organization.)

It was possible that Amelia might decide to give Neil and Sally the option to allow some portion of their "share" of inheritance to pass through the tax system. This she could do by bequeathing their shares in a form that would eventually be subject to tax— unless within 9 months of Amelia's death, Neil and/or Sally exercised **a qualified disclaimer** as to some or all of the taxable form of inheritance. In the appropriate estate plan documents, Amelia would specify that any property disclaimed by either Sally or Neil would automatically pass to the Roberts Family Fund, a donor-advised fund held and administered by the Community Foundation. Such property would qualify for the charitable estate tax deduction.

If Amelia had decided to take this approach, the final allocation between Personal Capital and Community Capital would be left to her children—the ultimate in family flexibility.

For the Roberts, flexibility had always been a vital part of Total Wealth Control.

Please see Graphic VI at the end of this Chapter for an overview of the Roberts' planning.

* * *

As they waited that May morning for their mother to enter the living room, Sally and Neil were curious, but not concerned. They fully respected Amelia's right to make all final decisions, and they had complete confidence in her wisdom. Perhaps their equanimity was also enhanced by the realization that all the planning done to date assured them of ample financial resources— just as their parents had intended.

This was the strategic flexibility of Total Wealth Control: a steady vision always poised for the ultimate possibility of no estate tax, but reserving the ability to modify the final outcome. After all, if the Roberts' various investments had not prospered, then it might have been critical to direct most or all of the property to the children and grandchildren— even though 50% or more would have been lost to taxes. The remaining 50% might have been essential to provide the Roberts heirs with adequate Personal Capital.

What if one of the children or grandchildren had developed serious medical problems, requiring enormous expense for care and treatment? No question— Total Wealth Control had to be flexible enough to meet the needs of the family first. Charity begins at home, as Amelia was fond of saying.

Fortunately for the Roberts, none of the "worst case" scenarios had happened. So now, on this warm May morning, Amelia had the luxury of choice, free from any concern for the financial well-being of her family.

Suddenly the room became very still...

TOTAL WEALTH CONTROL

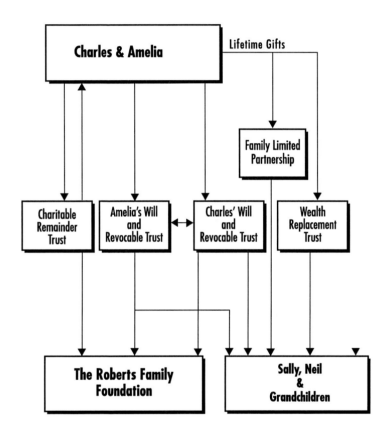

10 REVELATION AND INERTIA

As we have seen in the preceding pages, Charles and Amelia Roberts have made all of their planning decisions. **Now it is your turn.**

Having come this far, you may be curious or even inspired by the vision and techniques of the New Estate Planning. You are ready to learn more, and especially to learn what your version of the Vision might be.

Together with the sense of energy and purpose, you may also be feeling the pull of **inertia**. A voice is saying "This is too complicated," or "This kind of planning must be terribly expensive." There are so many other demands on your time and attention. Maybe it would be better to give all of this some thought before rushing into anything.

If you are having these or similar thoughts, that is entirely natural— but not necessarily to your advantage. <u>One thing is beyond question: if you simply maintain the status quo, your estate may be in enormous jeopardy. Uncle Sam has a plan for you.</u>

Let us briefly consider the practical problems that may deter you from pursuing the New Estate Planning.

First, the planning process involved in exploring,

designing and building Total Wealth Control is complex. However, if you are in a position to benefit from Total Wealth Control, you have already persevered through equally complex situations— building a business, developing a career, or understanding a web of extended family trusts, just to cite a few examples. You were able to move through those situations with your own motivation and persistence. *Through the process of the New Estate Planning, you can apply your skills to preserve and validate the benefits of earlier challenges.*

Is the process expensive? That depends on your perspective. When you compare the cost of the expert advice required to build a Zero Estate Tax Plan or any other version of Total Wealth Control, with the tax bill that would otherwise be looming over you and your family, you will readily see that you can generate a tremendous return on your investment in expertise.

To take one basic example, for spouses who have proper Wills and Revocable Trusts, and who have properly arranged their ownership of assets, the estate tax savings alone could exceed $750,000.

Beyond tax savings, what value do you place on your peace of mind? Or on the value of being able to reassure your children that you are thoroughly planning your estate?

Concern about complexity and cost can perhaps be tempered with this question: can you imagine anything more complex than the emotions of your son or daughter who must send the check to the Internal Revenue Service for an amount equal to one-half of your total estate— realizing that the check was totally unnecessary? What if you were the son or daughter?

* * *

Let me close with sincere appreciation for your interest and patience, and with a few words of advice concerning advisors.

First, if you wish to pursue any aspect of Total Wealth Control, please proceed with experts. Not only do the concepts require fluency in many aspects of estate and business planning, but when it comes to actually building the plan— drafting documents, selecting insurance, projecting taxes under different scenarios, managing assets and so forth— a thorough understanding of dense and shifting technical detail is absolutely essential to your success.

If you are looking for additional advisors, you may find helpful suggestions from your current advisors, family members, or your friends. In all events, you will be best served by advisors who combine technical competence, clear and open communication, and personal caring for you and your family.

Even if your current advisors do not possess all of the required expertise, that does not necessarily mean that they should have no role in the planning process. To the contrary, as they learn more about the New Estate Planning, their insights and skills may be extremely helpful to you and your team of other advisors. You will feel more comfortable making decisions if you can look your long-time, trusted advisors in the eye and ask: "Should I go ahead?" However, at least one member of your team must be an expert in this kind of planning, at the start of the journey.

How will you know whether your current advisors are equipped and prepared to work with you in the New Estate Planning? One suggestion: send each of them a copy of this book and ask for their comments. If they are open to new planning approaches, their initial response should involve more questions than answers. A good advisor is a good listener, to you and your new ideas. However, bear in mind that even for professional advisors there is a strong tendency to resist, avoid, or dismiss an unfamiliar approach. And of course not every aspect of Total Wealth Control will be appropriate for everyone. Flexible tailoring to your situation is critical.

What you need from your team of advisors is a full hearing, a creative and constructive dialogue which assures that there has been a collective grasp of Total Wealth Control. Then begins the painstaking and exhilarating process of building your Vision.

***

Calm seas and prosperous voyage.

GLOSSARY

In the language of the New Estate Planning, there are several key terms, many of which are used in this book. Once these terms have become familiar, they will serve you as very useful tools.

Annual Gift Exclusion, or Annual Gift. Each year you can make a gift of up to $11,000 to an unlimited number of individuals— without reducing your Unified Credit. Each Annual Gift may generate tax savings on the gift itself, plus growth in the value of the gift. Every year that you do not make such a gift, the opportunity is lost and gone forever.

Charitable Remainder Trust. A type of irrevocable trust that allows you to receive distributions for the rest of your life, and typically the life of your spouse. The distributions are derived from the sale and reinvestment of property that you (the "Donor") transfer to the Trust as a gift. The Charitable Remainder Trust pays no tax on the income derived from the sale or investment of its assets. When you and your spouse have both died, the distributions cease and the remaining Trust property is distributed to one or more charitable organizations chosen by you (and/or your spouse), including a Family Foundation.

Family Foundation. A special form of charitable organization that is exempt from federal and state income tax. A Family Foundation may be controlled by the members of one family. With Total Wealth Control, the Family Foundation is one choice for the charitable organization that will receive some portion or all of the assets that would otherwise be subject to estate tax.

Family Limited Partnership. Formed in accordance with local state law, this type of partnership typically has the parents acting as the general or controlling partners. The children, or trusts for their benefit, are typically the Limited Partners. The parents make gifts of the Limited Partner Interests to the children, preferably in trust. Since the value of these Limited Partner Interests may be substantially discounted for gift tax purposes, the Family Limited Partnership enables parents to maintain control of valuable property, while at the same time shifting a significant portion of the assets away from potential taxes or creditor claims.

In most states, the **Limited Liability Company** is available as an alternative to the Family Limited Partnership.

Generation-Skipping Transfer Tax. A federal tax, at a rate equal to the highest estate tax rate, imposed upon property that passes from one person to another person who is more than one generation younger than the person transferring the property. Example: Grandparent transfers property to

Grandchild.

Generation-Skipping Transfer Tax ("GST") Exemption. The value of property that may be passed to a beneficiary who is two or more generations younger than the transferor, without triggering the GST; currently, the amount of the exemption is $1,500,000 per transferor.

Glossary. A well-meaning attempt to provide approximate meanings for complex terms, furnished with the caveat that there is no such thing as an accurate generalization.

Irrevocable Life Insurance Trust. A legal arrangement created primarily for the purpose of owning insurance on the life of the person(s) who created the Trust. If the Trust is properly designed and administered, the death benefit from the insurance will not be subject to tax in the estates of the insured person, his or her spouse, and one or more generations of younger heirs.

Total Wealth Control. The goal of the New Estate Planning, Total Wealth Control, flows from the realization that it is not possible to pass all of your wealth directly to your children or other heirs without losing 50% or more of the wealth in the form of taxes. However, with Total Wealth Control it is possible to replace the tax with a charitable gift, which can be structured as an integral part of the legacy to the children. The choice is yours.

Gift and Estate Tax Exclusions. You may transfer up to $1,000,000 by gift during your lifetime, or $1,500,000 at death— with no tax liability. With proper planning, a husband and wife should be able to "shelter" or protect a total of $3,000,000 in assets from any tax liability. The Estate Tax Exclusion is scheduled to increase to $2,000,000 in 2006.

Unlimited Gift or Estate Tax Charitable Deduction. Property transferred during your lifetime and/or at your death to a qualified charitable organization, including a Family Foundation, will be completely sheltered from any transfer tax.

Unlimited Marital Gift or Estate Tax Deduction. Property transferred from one spouse to another, either during lifetime or upon death, will generally qualify for a deduction for federal gift and estate tax purposes. The marital deduction is unlimited, so that with proper planning there will be no tax due on the death of the first spouse. However, all property that qualified for the marital deduction will ordinarily be subject to gift or estate tax when it is transferred by the surviving spouse.

Personal Capital Trust. A form of irrevocable trust funded with gifts of property that will not be subject to estate tax. It is often used in place of the term "Irrevocable Life Insurance Trust," although a Personal Capital Trust may hold assets other than or in addition to an insurance policy.

The primary purpose of a Personal Capital Trust is to help assure one form of inheritance for your children or other heirs— their Personal Capital— by replacing property that would either be taken by the government in the form of estate taxes, or else given to one or more family charities as part of Total Wealth Control.

The Trust may also provide the Trust assets with significant protection against divorce or other types of claims.

Zero Estate Tax Plan. A version of Total Wealth Control built on the premise that if you have substantial wealth, you can choose your own form of Community Capital: heavy estate taxes, or charitable gift. Upon this premise, you and your advisors create a flexible array of estate and business planning arrangements that enable you to provide the desired amount and form of inheritance for your children and other heirs, while maintaining the desired level of family control over that portion of your estates that is earmarked for public or social benefits.

The Zero Estate Tax Plan will result in no federal or state estate tax being paid. The Plan may also eliminate capital gains tax, and the double tax on retirement plans.

Acknowledgements

The writing and publication of this guide have been made possible by so many people and organizations that a complete acknowledgement of their contributions is unfortunately not possible. Nevertheless, in the evolution of *Beyond Death & Taxes*, there are two contributions that I would like to mention.

I was introduced to the choice between Voluntary Philanthropy and Involuntary Philanthropy by Renaissance, Inc., an organization based in Carmel, Indiana, that is devoted to giving techniques, particularly the Charitable Remainder Trust.

I was introduced to Renaissance by John Balis, a professional colleague and insurance agent with whom I have shared much of the voyage of discovery reflected in this guide. John also contributed many helpful comments on the text, and the use of graphics.

* * *

Without the open minds and confidence of many clients and their dedicated advisors, the planning concepts put forth in these pages would be mere abstractions. With their questions, creativity, and enthusiasm, our clients transform ideals into action— and new challenge.

About the Author

Gregory J. Englund is a tax attorney who practices law in Boston, Massachusetts.

Mr. Englund is a graduate of Swarthmore College (1969) and Harvard Law School (1974). He holds a Masters Degree in Taxation from Boston University School of Law (1979). He served for two years with the Peace Corps in Cameroon, West Africa.

Mr. Englund works with clients and their other advisors to help clients build, preserve, and enjoy their wealth. His areas of concentration include business and estate planning for owners of family or other closely-held businesses, and planning for the next generation of owners.

Mr. Englund is a member of the Massachusetts Bar.

Also available:

Seasons of Decision, A Practical Guide to Life's Important Financial and Legal Decisions. (178 pages; June 2000)